Seriously—Cancer?
I Do Not Have Time for This!

Lauren Graham

Inspiring Voices®
A Service of **Guideposts**

Inspiring Voices books may be ordered through booksellers or by contacting:

Inspiring Voices
1663 Liberty Drive
Bloomington, IN 47403
www.inspiringvoices.com
1-(866) 697-5313

ISBN: 978-1-4624-0601-2 (sc)
ISBN: 978-1-4624-0602-9 (e)

Library of Congress Control Number: 2013907424

Printed in the United States of America.

Inspiring Voices rev. date: 6/3/2013

Prologue

We had a good thing going. A comfortable, lasting marriage, wonderful kids, a challenging job and lots of friends. What more could anyone ask for? I was proud of the life that we had made and knew that God had been overly generous when pouring His blessings out on us. It seemed as if nothing could hurt us. Until it did. When the tornado in our lives hit, nothing could have prepared us for the fear, the heartache, the shock that we felt.

When Lauren told me that her lymph nodes were swollen in April, I did what I had always done as her mother, went about fixing it. I took her to the doctor, and she prescribed some antibiotics. We went about our normal routines. When the antibiotics were gone but the swollen lymph nodes weren't, I knew that something wasn't right. We went back to the doctor who then decided to run some labs and refer us to an ear, nose, and throat specialist. When she made a casual comment in the office about a young woman she had treated who had presented to her with swollen lymph nodes that turned out to be lymphoma, I got angry. I didn't want anything to be wrong with MY daughter, and I didn't want to hear of anything bad. All of my nursing experience and knowledge led me to believe that what was going on with Lauren was not "normal," but I wanted to rationalize it into something minor. When we saw the ENT, I tried to convince him that it was probably mono or cat scratch fever. He assured us that it was neither, but gave us a sense of relief when he suggested a wait and see attitude for a probable virus that would run its course.

I was being overly optimistic, probably in denial, that everything was fine. After all, she looked fine, felt fine, and was just her normal self. When more lymph nodes became visibly swollen overnight a couple of weeks later, I started worrying. We went back to the doctor who scheduled a biopsy for that week. It was looking more and more like this was not something that I could "fix." The doctor continued to be pretty laid back and assured us by telling us that he felt that it was going to be viral. When he returned from the surgery, he dropped the bomb. He said that the pathologist was giving him "no good news." He said that there were only two possibilities - autoimmune disease or lymphoma. I was in shock. I started bargaining with God, praying for an autoimmune disease. I couldn't imagine my daughter having cancer. How would we deal with something like this? How could I face the possibility of losing her? Because Lauren was sedated after the surgery, the doctor didn't tell her what he found. We went home, and I told Robert that we couldn't talk about the possibilities. I guess I thought that if we didn't talk about it, it wouldn't be real. I didn't want to scare her, and I was too scared myself to let myself talk out loud about it. That Saturday night, I finally told Lauren what it looked like we were facing. She surprised me when she said, "I hope that it is lymphoma and not an autoimmune disease." I was shocked to hear this. Cancer was a life-threatening disease. I had just lost my grandmother to lung cancer five months earlier. In my mind, cancer was just too scary to face. When I asked her why, she said, "Because if it is cancer, there is a possibility that it can be cured. If it is an autoimmune disease, I will deal with it the rest of my life." That was the beginning of the fighting attitude that would sustain her through this challenge.

The following Monday, the doctor called and said that he had a diagnosis. It was Memorial Day, so the office was closed. He

2

said that he would be waiting there for us. Lauren and I went by ourselves. He came right out and said, "Do you want the good news or the bad news first?" I braced myself, knowing that our lives would forever be changed in this moment. He said, "You have a nasty disease, but it can be cured. But only with an all-out, full-court press, MD Anderson, the whole bit." He went on to tell us that the diagnosis was T- cell precursor lymphoblastic lymphoma. That might as well have been a foreign language to us, but a language that we would quickly come to understand and speak ourselves.

Tragedy affects many families. Mine had been no different. All of my grandparents gone and most of them after months or years of serious illnesses. My brother killed accidently at age 19. My biological father taken much too soon the month before I was born. I guess all of these things in my life prepared me for what would transpire. The examples set before me by my parents as they dealt with the care giving duties for their parents through serious illness, the loss of their son, and the loss of their spouses made them stronger. I always looked on tragedies such as these with sympathy. I thought about how hard it must be to deal with things almost too hard to face. I thought I could empathize with them. I now know that before this experience, I had no clue as to how hard it can be to deal with serious illness in someone you love, especially your child. It completely turns your life upside down. It allows you no control. It scares the life out of you. It makes you physically sick. Someone you love more than yourself is seriously ill, and you can do nothing to stop it. You are not able to go back to the days where illness was not an issue. You would take it all on yourself if only you could. Your heart aches for the pain and suffering that you see your loved one go through. People cannot understand how you feel, but they can help. Many helped us. They helped us with their prayers; they helped us with shoulders to cry on; they helped us with the financial burden that this placed on us. They went out of their way to be there for us, whatever it took. It

3

is still amazing to me how many angels are out there. All of them sent by God to provide for us what we needed when we needed it. Things we didn't even know to ask for, God provided before we realized that we needed them.

We can now look back and see how this experience has changed our lives. We still have a good life, in fact, a great life. We have a Mighty God who knows our prayers before we pray them. He has known every step of the way what would happen to Lauren. As scary as each treatment, ER visit, hospitalization, and surgery was, He has brought her through each one of them safely. He has given us all strength to do what we had to do. He has calmed our fears when we cried out. He has directed our path when we didn't know what to do. He has allowed us to wake up each day ready to face whatever we have to, even when the day might be scary.

God has given me more patience, more spontaneity, more compassion for others. He has made me strong and assertive when I needed to be. He has made me quiet and passive when I needed to be. He has directed my actions every moment. He has made me trust Him more. My faith is stronger now. Maybe that was part of this trial for me. I needed to learn how to trust Him and let go. When I could do nothing but cry out to Him, He was there for me. He is always in control.

Lauren Christine Graham. My firstborn, my only daughter, my love. What can I say about her? She is the strongest person I know. She is beautiful, inside and out. She is funny, resilient, and headstrong. She amazes me every day. How could I have known that her headstrong ways as a child would be necessary for her to remain tough in facing this challenge? She reaches out and comforts me when I can't hide my fear anymore. She makes me a better person. She is always sharing her faith through her actions. She is an inspiration. She says that she doesn't deserve the credit, that it is God working through her, but she is an inspiration. God has chosen her. His light shines through her. God has changed us

4

all by using her. I love her more than she could ever imagine and thank her for being the wonderful daughter that she is.

–Laurie Graham, Lauren's Mom

God is within her, she will not fail.
God will help her at the break of day. Psalm 46:5.

Sometimes, you just need to get out how you feel. When I was diagnosed with cancer three weeks before my twenty-first birthday, I was shocked. I had just figured out what I was going to major in after three years in college, was having the time of my life with my friends, and had just started a new relationship with the man of my dreams. How does something so simple, a swollen lymph node, turn into *cancer*?

I figure that you only have two options. You are either going to be the negative patient who constantly wonders, "Why me?" or you are going to be the person who puts on her big-girl panties and says, "Ok cancer, let's duke this out. You and me." I figured out really quickly that option one just wouldn't work for me. Attitude has so much to do with the treatment process. Some of you may read this and think, "Well what about all those people who had great attitudes but still died? What about them?" I still believe that God gives people the attitude for a reason. If people can see that, regardless of what is happening in your life you still have a good attitude, it will inspire them. It inspires me.

I had a lot of difficulty finding books or articles about people my age who had been diagnosed. My type of illness wasn't classified as a childhood cancer because, at twenty-one, I was an adult – but I sure didn't feel like one! It's a weird stage to be in. You learn to deal with issues that are way before your time, such as infertility, heart attack-like chest pains, bone and muscle pains, the list goes on. Although this "book" is just a compilation of e-mails I wrote, encouraging e-mails or just thoughts from me, it helped me through the rough times. I highly recommend the act of writing of journaling for anyone going through a situation similar to mine. Believe it or not, people want to know how you are. If I can help one person by putting this together, then my work is done. I hope you enjoy.

Sunday, June 3, 2007

Subject: Testing!

Hello all!!

So, I'm testing this out, seeing how the mass email thing will work. Most of you know by this point, but I finally got an appointment at M.D. Anderson on Tuesday!! Super excited to go and get that done and over with. Tuesday will just be a lot of testing and scans. I'm so thrilled (sarcastic much?). I'm going to TRY and keep everyone updated on how I am doing, whether it be every couple of days or weeks, not exactly sure yet. We expect to be in Houston for two to three weeks (don't forget to call me on the 19th and say HAPPY BIRTHDAY!!!). Hopefully I can start chemo by the end of the week so these darn lymph nodes will get smaller!

Another note-thanks to Jamie's momma we found out that the color for lymphoma is lime green. Neat huh? If I'm going to have cancer, at least I have a cool color. So wear lots of lime green and think of me!!!

This entire week has been unbelievably hectic, and I can't thank everyone enough for helping out!! Thanks for helping me move out of the apartment (record time, two hours!), the flowers, gifts, and cards. It's like my birthday, but super early! I love the support, so ya'll better not stop because it makes me feel better!

As far as how I am feeling now, I honestly feel fine. Other than being tired (taking two hour naps when I insist I'm only going to take a thirty minute nap), the only thing that is bothering me now is the lymph nodes that are pressing on certain nerves. The one under my arm (aka Pity) presses on nerves in my arm, which hurts and then we think that the ones in my legs are pressing on other nerves. They are just getting in my way if anything. I'm not concerned at all about the entire process I am about to face. I

7

know that I will get through it just fine, and it's definitely a neat learning process. Eventually, it will go away.

Last but not least in this email, a lot of you know that the absolute hardest part of this whole process for me is knowing I am going to lose my hair. Not to be conceited (ok, maybe a little bit) but I LOVE my hair. It listens to me and does what I want it to! But, all good things must eventually end, so, with the help of my great friend Megan, I cut ten inches off today. Very sad. Everyone seems to like it though, and my head doesn't weigh forty-five pounds when I get out of the shower now! Yay!!! We are going to try and make something out of my own hair, and if it not send it off to Locks of Love.

With that said...I promise pictures of the new hair soon (It's short!), and more than likely the next email will be on either Tuesday night or Wednesday. Keep in touch with me; I'm sure the computer will keep me occupied! It's so much easier than the cell phone, especially now! Love you all....

Lauren

● ● ● ● ● ● ● ●

Wednesday, June 6, 2007

Subject: And here's another update

Hola everyone!!!

Oh what a busy past few days. Delightful. Let me just give you a rundown of it all.

So yesterday was the big day! I finally had an appointment with the doctors there. We started the day off with vital signs and getting my blood drawn. I felt like I gave a donation. *Seventeen* vials of blood!! Walked around in amazement most of the day, that hospital is insane. They have aquariums in the hospital!! Neat huh? I also had a bone marrow aspiration done, and I tell you what, I would be perfectly happy to *never* have that again.

Bad news is, I will. The reason why they do the bone marrow deal is to determine if the cancer cells are in the bone marrow. They numb up your hip, stick a needle down into the bone, extract bone marrow, and then chip off a piece of the bone. I told the nurse right off the bat, "I'm a wuss and I want lots of pain medication!!!!!" It feels like a huge charlie horse times a million in the back of your leg and butt and everywhere else, ugh. Not fun. I'll have to keep having those because they did find 30% of these cells in my bone marrow. Sad day.

So, what does that mean? Basically, I have the same thing, but throw leukemia on there too. The reason why it is lymphoma also is because it pretty much originated in my lymph nodes. Therefore, it's Stage 4 (which is the worst in this case). So my official diagnosis is Acute Lymphoblastic Lymphoma/Leukemia, also known as ALL.

Then today! Ugh. Don't even get me started. We were supposed to go to the zoo to see the rest of my family, but nooooooo. We

9

had to wait an hour and a half to watch an 8-minute video on the central line. So dumb.

So, tomorrow I have a pretty busy day. I get my central line put in (basically an IV in my chest that will stay put for a while), then I have a PET scan, which will find my pets...wait no, to see if there are any other problems in my body, meet with my doctor, and have my first round of chemo. Yay. P.S, that will be in my spine. Gross.

The chemo should work like this, we think. First week, three different types of drugs plus the dose in my spine. I'll get chemo through my spine and chest. Each week for the next 3-4 weeks I will have two drugs through my central line. At the end of those four weeks, the cancer will be re-staged and if I'm doing well, I can come home! I can do most of the treatment at home; they just want me to stay in Houston to make sure everything goes ok.

So! That's the down low. That's what I know, that's the latest. More than likely, we won't be able to come home for about a month. I'm telling you though, July 3, I have to be better! I have a Keith Urban concert to go to!

Thank you so much everyone for keeping in touch with me and responding. It's so nice to open my email and see all the well-wishes from everyone. Love you all, see ya soon!

P.S...A lot of you may know, but I keep a little book with prayers and quotes and what not in it. I have relied on this a lot in the past few weeks. I figure what the hay, I can share some if it with you!! Any objections, just let me know.

"Give up for ONE second and that is where you will finish it."
–Unknown

"While we may not be able to control all that happens to us, we can control what happens inside us."- Benjamin Franklin

"You earn God's ear by telling him not what you know, but what you DON'T know."–Unknown

Love choooo all!
Lauren

• • • • • • • •

Saturday June 9, 2007

Subject: Sorry I didn't spell check I'm lazy!

Grrr. I wrote out the entire email and then it got erased.

Ok, so anywho, the last few days have been very busy! I had my central line put in, which hurt like heck. I had my PET scan, which wasn't too great either. You have to lay flat in a room for an hour, and the walls are paper thin. The man in the room next to me was snoring at the top of his lungs. Awesome.

Yesterday I had my first round of chemo in my spine (that wasn't too bad), and then about 10 minutes ago I had my first round through my IV. Not too bad. I've been admitted to the hospital for the next few days just to see how I react to the chemo.

Here is how the chemo works. I go through the induction phase which has five different drugs, but I'm not even going to try and name them! On the 15th day of chemo I have another bone marrow aspiration (Yay!). If there are less than 5% of the cancer cells in my bone marrow then I can go onto the next phase of chemo. Including induction, there are, I think, 5 stages? The chemo that they are giving me is the same type that they give to pediatric patients. I'm the 16th patient here to get this treatment in my age group. That's cool.

One of my big concerns with this whole deal was whether or not I would be able to have kids once the chemo was all said and done. If I went through chemo without doing anything, I would have an 80% chance of becoming infertile. No bueno, no good. I ended up getting a shot of a medicine called Lupron. It puts me into pre-menopause. How many twenty year olds can say that they went into pre-menopause? The ongoing joke between me and my mom is that everyone better watch out, Lauren is going to have hot flashes and road rage!! Stay away!

Sean and Eric (my boyfriend and my brother) came into town last night. They both busted into the hospital wearing lime green. Those are my boys.

Bad news: I don't think I get to go to Keith Urban. The doctors say crowds are bad. I might just sneak in though.

Thanks to everyone who sends gifts, cards, emails, keep them coming. It definitely keeps me in high spirits!! Here are some more quotes, some of these are songs, verses, sayings, things that make me happy! Keep in touch.

Love chooooooo allllllllllll.....*Lauren*

"If your confidence comes from God, anything is possible." –Unknown

"Instead of saying, I'm going to quit this, say I'm going to START this."–Unknown

"Christianity is so much more than being faithful; salvation is every day, not just once a week."–Unknown

"Laugh your heart out, dance in the rain, cherish the memories, ignore the pain, love and learn, forget and forgive, because remember you only have one life to live."–Unknown

And my favorite...

"You'll never become old and wise if you aren't young and crazy!" –Unknown

• • • • • • •

Sunday June 10, 2007

Subject: Quick update!

So I have been in the hospital since Friday, but good news!!

They ran my blood work this morning and the blast cells (the stupid bad ugly cancer cells) came down by 10%!! When they first did my blood work, the count was at 13% and this morning they were at 3%. WHOOOOOO HOOOOOOOOOO!!

Bad news is that the steroid they are making me take is making my blood sugar kind of go out of whack, so my blood sugar is higher than normal, which means I have to have my blood sugar checked four times a day and get an insulin shot four times a day. Grr. I hate shots. They are giving me 90 milligrams of this steroid a day, so watch out. I can beat you up.

But that is the good news!! And I get discharged tomorrow!! And my stupid lymph nodes that have been driving me crazy are finally shrinking!

That's all folks. Eventually the chemo will make me sicker, but right now I don't care because my lymph node enemies are finally getting the hint that I don't like them.

Love chooooo all!
Lauren

"Before I go off on what you SHOULD and SHOULD NOT do, I'll start with what I did. I grew up knowing that God exists. A lot of people think that this is enough...IT'S NOT. Acknowledging Him is not having a relationship with Him."–Unknown

"Believe nothing just because a so-called wise person said it... Believe nothing just because a belief is generally held....

Believe nothing just because it's said in ancient books.....
Believe nothing just because it's said to be of divine origin....
Believe nothing just because someone else believes it....
Believe only what you yourself test and judge to be true."
–Buddha

"Scripture says that we are a family, it doesn't matter how old or young we are-break the boundaries."–Unknown

"Do not be overcome by evil, but overcome evil with good."
Romans 12:21(NIV)

• • • • • • • •

Wednesday June 11, 2007

Subject: I know you crazy people miss me.

What a week! We finally have time to sit and do nothing. No treatment today, no treatment tomorrow, ahhhhh. No more needles and pokes and blah. So far, everything is going really well. The blast cells that were at 13% when we started are now down to zero! Pretty cool huh? Go Lauren cells for beating those up. My PET scan showed that the cancer hasn't spread anywhere other than where we figured it was (the lymph nodes). The lymph node under my arm that gave me so many problems was 3.3 cm by 3.3 cm, but it's gone! I can't even feel Betsy or Pity or any of those other trouble makers anymore. So very, very cool.

I got through the one chemo that they were worried I would have an allergic reaction to with no reactions! The medicine is called Pegulated Aspariginase. Who comes up with these names? We just have been calling it Asparagus. So far I haven't had too many crazy side effects, just some headaches, being sleepy, the usual. If chemo keeps up like this, I'll be fine! Also, the chemo that I am on won't drop my white blood cell counts down as much as other chemotherapies, which means I am less prone to infection and less anemic. Also less chance of a transfusion! Super excited, so you all know what this means, more chances for Keith Urban! And hopefully heading up to camp for like, a day, and going home!

I am amazed by the outpouring of support and kindness from people I don't even know. The fact that so many of you would offer things that I can't even dream of, and people care and support me when they don't even know me is simply fantabulous.

A lot of people are asking about my schedule next week, so here it is, at least what we know. I have another round of chemo on Friday at 8:30, so that will last a few hours, and then on Monday the 18th, I have another lumbar puncture with some more chemo, more lab work (blah). On the 19th I have more lab work and a doctor's appointment, and then the 22nd I have more lab work, a bone marrow aspiration (gross) and more chemo. They were trying to make me have some type of treatment on the 19th, and I said no way, don't you know what day that is?! So, next week, Tuesday, Wednesday, and Thursday are all days off! At least, we think so. Hopefully everything will be good with the bone marrow aspiration; if it is less than 5% we are doing fabulous and can move on to the next round of treatment in a few weeks!

I'm getting scatterbrained with my quotes, so I never remember what I write and what I didn't write. I find a lot of help in songs, and those who know me know I love music. So if I have song lyrics as a quote, deal with it! Love choo all!

Lauren

"Your talent is God's gift to you, what you do with it is your gift back to God."–Leo Buscaglia

"I praise you because I am FEARFULLY and WONDERFULLY made; your works are wonderful and I know that full well." Psalm 139:14 (NIV)

"Live life without fear, confront all obstacles and know that you can overcome them."–Unknown

"Don't worry about anything; instead pray about everything. Tell God what you need, and thank Him for all He has done." Philippians 4:6 (NIV)

"Come let us sing a song, a song declaring we belong to Jesus- He's all we need...

Lift up a heart of praise; sing now with voices raised to Jesus-Sing to the King."
–Billy James Foote-"Sing to the King"

"And though I can't understand why this happened
I know that I will when I look back someday
And see how You've brought beauty from ashes
And made me gold purified through these flames..."
–Songwriters: Max Hsu/Tricia Brock Baumhardt; Performed by Superchick-"Beauty from Pain"

That's all folks! Miss you all like crazy!

• • • • • • • •

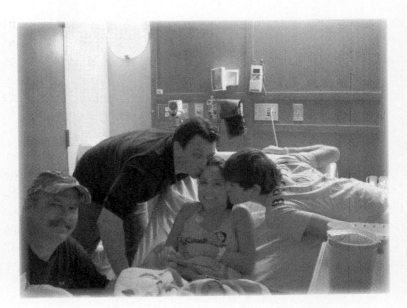

Thursday, June 14, 2007

Subject: So we had a bad day.

Well, it was bound to happen. We finally had a bad day.

The side effects of everything are finally starting to present themselves. Darn it. One of my main problems is not being able to walk very well. I get winded super quickly and have a really hard time getting around. Another weird effect is my jaw, it's crazy! Imagine chewing gum for hours on end as fast as you possibly can and then imagine how your jaw feels the next day. Ouch! I finally ended up taking a painkiller for it, which says a lot because I can't stand the pills I take now.

We finally got to go to the zoo today, but it was a short lived trip. Probably not the smartest idea to be out in the heat, but it was so much fun! My cousin Jackie (who is *very* pregnant) went with us today. Me and my mom were saying how funny would it be if she had the baby there at the zoo? She'll be a great mom!

Anyways, on top of everything the past few days, when we got home from the zoo today, Sean (my fabulous boyfriend) called my mom asking about a cut on his hand and whether or not he should go to the emergency room. He has to have surgery tomorrow on his left thumb - ending up tearing a tendon. NO BUENO!

So, I'm about sick of taking medicine (up to 16 pills a day! whoo hooo!), my friends are in Corpus, I miss home, and when my boyfriend gets hurt I can't take care of him. Overall it was kind of a bummer past few days. So please keep everyone in your prayers, especially my parents and my brother and Sean and his surgery. I know all of them have a hard time with this, but it will be ok.

I have another chemo treatment in the morning, so hopefully I won't feel too sick after everything. Sleep is definitely becoming a very good friend of mine.

On the up and up, my girls are coming into town this weekend (and hopefully Sean, if he isn't all doped up on medicine), so we have lots of shopping planned!

You sometimes begin to wonder, why in the world did this happen to me? I'm 20 years old, right in the middle of everything, and *bam*, cancer decides it wants to be my friend. I was thinking about it last night and it just hit me-there is *nothing* I can do to stop it. I can ask all the questions, how did this happen, why lymphoma, and I will never have the answers for that. Although I am still in a positive mind set, it is very frustrating to go from being an independent person to having to be pushed around in a wheelchair when all you want to do is walk and be yourself again. I keep telling myself that all this is happening for whatever reason, and I'm sure I will figure it out eventually. So keep up the encouraging emails, keep me smiling!

Ok, so this wasn't the most eventful email, but I don't feel too great right now and that bed is screaming my name because it wants me to sleep in it. Miss you all, can't wait to see you!

Love chooo alll...
Lauren

• • • • • • • •

Monday June 18, 2007

Subject: Anyone miss me yet?

Well, today is going to be a long day.

I have more appointments this morning, and another round of a new type of chemo that will be given to me through my spine. Yay. The past few days I have been kind of down and a little bit unhappy just because of all the side effects that are kicking in and messing with my body. It becomes harder and harder to sleep at night for so many different reasons, whether it be the unstoppable night sweats (gross, I know!), or the pressure buildup in my jaw and ears. Despite all of this, I still am trying to remain positive not only for myself but for those around me. So, wish me luck today with my chemo and everything else! And thank you so much to everyone who has already made my birthday an awesome day, even though it technically isn't here yet! As you go on through your day, think about these little thoughts I'm going to leave you with. Granted, two of them are songs, but I don't care. They make me happy. I hope everyone has a fantabulous day, love choo all! Can't wait to see you!

Lauren

"Don't stop, thinking about tomorrow
Don't stop, it'll soon be here
It'll be better than before,
yesterday's gone, yesterday's gone"
–Songwriters: Christine McVie/John McVie ; Performed by Fleetwood Mac-"Don't Stop"

Finally, I leave you with one of my absolute favorite scriptures. I know I have shared this with some of you before, but to me if truly captures the essence of how we should live our lives every day.

"Do you not know? Have you not heard? The Lord is the everlasting God, the Creator of the ends of the earth. He will not grow tired or weary, and his understanding no one can fathom. He gives strength to the weary and increases the power of the weak. Even youths grow tired and weary, and young men stumble and fall; but those who hope in the Lord will renew their strength. They will soar on wings like eagles; they will run and not grow weary, they will walk and not be faint." Isaiah 40:28-31(NIV)

I love that verse so much because it proves to me and everyone else that *no one* can understand the depth of His understanding, and that He gives power to those who understand that they have *no* power.

Miss choo all, can't wait to see ya!

• • • • • • • •

Wednesday June 20, 2007

Subject: Hello again from me

Well the birthday has come and passed, and I tell you what, I slept through most of it. Way to ring in 21 huh? I started thinking about all the reasons why I was excited to turn 21, and how everything just becomes so increasingly trivial during these times.

In all honesty, I was thrilled to turn 21 for a ton of reasons. To be able to go out with my friends and not be the one person who had the big M's on her hands that stood for minor, to be able to have the freedom to order a drink if I wanted to, to maybe not feel quite so left out in a sense. But you know what? 21 is just a number.

As a lay here in bed, officially 21, the only thing that crosses my mind is how naive or insensitive it was for me to focus on those things when there is so much going on around me. I never in a million years thought or even felt that people I don't even know would care enough about me to send me birthday wishes, or birthday cards, presents, words of encouragement. The list goes on and on. I received well over a hundred emails in the course of the past three days, and some people say they have met me, and some say they haven't. I don't do names well to begin with, so I'm excited to get back home and put faces to all of the names that I have "met' through email in the past few weeks.

Those who know me know that I am a child of God. I love Jesus Christ with all of my heart and all of my soul, and I know that everyone has a point in their life where sometimes they just question their faith, or wonder why things happen. I could have spent the past few weeks angry and upset, or mad that I had to spend my birthday getting chemo into my spine, but you know what? I'm not mad. I'm not angry. This whole process has happened to open up my eyes so much and to realize that despite everything, I still need to keep my priorities strait. (Someone once told me that you know you are from Texas when you spell strait like...a.k.a. George Strait). In this whole process, if people can keep their eyes open and realize that God is still in control, and that He still has a huge master plan for everyone, no matter what it is, then that makes me a happier person. A lot of the time we miss our opportunities to take on God because we are too "busy." Don't take for granted waking up for church on Sunday morning or stop reading your Bible just because it is something that is always there. I can't even express to you how much I would love to be in a church right now, listening and learning about the things God has to offer me. It should be like that for everyone. God is always there, and I forget who I heard it from, but someone once said that you can never be a good student if you are not being in the word. So even if you just sit and acknowledge the fact that God is there for you whenever you need Him, I like to think that God needs US to give Him feedback and let Him know how much we appreciate the things He does for us. Luis, my youth pastor, sent me a great bible verse today that really helped me so I'm going share it with you.

"God is within her, she will not fall; God will help her at the break of day." Psalm 46:5 (NIV)

With all that said I will give you an update of the past few days. On Monday I was supposed to have a lumbar puncture with the chemo, but my blood was clotting too slowly. I had good clotting factors, but the doctors didn't want to risk giving me the lumbar puncture (LP) so instead they gave a transfusion of some big long word I can't say. We went in at 1:30, got called into the room at 2:30, were told at 3:30 they wouldn't do the LP, and then 3 hours later they finally gave me the transfusion. So, because of that they really had no choice but to push the LP to Tuesday (the big 21!). We were hoping that it would be just a morning affair, but it ended up being pretty much an all day thing. Oh well, have fun with it. The good thing is that Memaw and Popeye came up, and Sean was here also, and while I was opening my birthday presents I was so heavily medicated that I don't remember half of the things I got so that just means I get to go through everything again and relive my birthday glory.

So thanks again to everyone who has made my birthday memorable. I have a huge pile of gifts that are sitting in the corner whenever I am ready to tackle them! I love chooo all so very much, and I don't know what I would do without the continuous support of my family and friends. Hopefully I can see you all soon!

Quotes of the day...

"But if we are the body, why aren't His arms reaching?
Why aren't His hands healing?
Why aren't His words teaching?
Why is His love not showing them-there is a way...."
–Songwriter Mark Hal; Performed by Casting Crowns-"If We are the Body"

"Be joyful always; pray continually; give thanks in all circumstances, for this is God's will for you in Christ Jesus. Do not put out the Spirit's fire; do not treat prophecies with contempt. Test everything. Hold onto the good. Avoid every kind of evil." 1 Thessalonians 5:16-22(NIV)

"I woke up this morning, with this feeling inside me that I can't explain
Like a weight that I'd carried been carried away, away...
–Songwriters: Wayne Hector/Stephen Robson; Performed by Rascal Flatts-"Feels Like Today"

• • • • • • •

Sunday June 24, 2007

Subject: Update from the crazy girl

All right folks here is the latest update.

I have been asleep for the past three days, yet last night I didn't sleep at all. That seems to be my latest problem; it's kind of a bummer because sleeping helps so much because it just passes the time, but not today. I'm also having a lot of problems eating, but only because I am starving and end up eating way too fast and then I get sick. Anyways, this email is not going to be very long because I'm sleepy and I just thought I would check in with everyone. Please keep sending the encouraging emails, I love them!

One huge prayer request. We need the cells in my bone marrow to be less than five percent. I had my biopsy this past Friday, and if it's less than five percent then I can go onto the next round of chemo, but if not, I have to redo this induction all over, which would not be good! So please pray for that. I love you all, miss you like crazy, and can't wait to see you!

Lauren

"I gain strength, courage, and confidence by every experience in which I must stop and look fear in the face...I say to myself, I've lived through this and I can take the next thing that comes along."
–Eleanor Roosevelt

• • • • • • • •

Tuesday June 26, 2007

Subject: YAYYYYYYYYY!!!!

Great news! The bone marrow is less than 5%!!!! 2% to be exact, doctor says that it looks like a remission type deal already, which is so super exciting. I'm definitely becoming more and more depressed the longer that we are here because I want to go home, but I know I have to be here in Houston at least another week. If all goes well we can come home in a couple of weeks.

We had a scare yesterday and had to go the emergency room. I had some type of reaction to the nausea medication I was taking; it was almost like a mini-seizure. Kind of scary. It was just like severe muscle spasms but in my neck. They called it a "dystonic reaction." No more compazine for me! So this is the latest, short but sweet. Keep the prayers up, they lift my spirits more than you can imagine!

Love choo allllllll

Lauren

"God knows what you need when you need it."–Unknown

"Just like we prepare meals for guests...we need to prepare ourselves for God. We need to "clean house" before we come into God's presence."–Unknown

• • • • • • • •

Friday June 29, 2007

Subject: Here's a new update!

All right everyone, the initial chemo is DONE! I've been through my four rounds of induction, we made it! Today was a little bit rough, but I actually got some sleep, which is super awesome. Pray for me next week, lots of stuff is coming up. My white blood counts are back up again which is super good (6.6 I think?)...last week they were in the 3's. Keith Urban is on Tuesday, so hopefully all goes well and we can make it to the concert. Ticketmaster is being really good about everything (so far) and we get to go into the concert an hour earlier. Maybe I can get a pretty cool shirt huh?

Moving on, next Thursday is a big day for me. I have more blood work, another PET scan, another bone marrow aspiration, and another lumbar puncture. I'll need prayers on that day. It's going to be a rough one. That PET scan is no fun because you can't eat for 6 hours before hand, so maybe they can just knock me out for everything huh?

Oh ya, sad news, the hair is definitely coming out. My guess is that by the end of next week the majority of it will be gone, but it's ok! I'm coming to terms with it. Eric bought me this awesome Little Mermaid wig that is bright red that I seriously plan on wearing everywhere.

Dad and Eric came into town yesterday! It was so good to finally see them again. Dad fixed up the house for me with air purifiers and stuff so I don't get sick, but they will probably go home soon so they can finish getting the house in order for me. Pray for my dog Brownie too, we know that she is very lonely.

Anyways, that is my physical update.

As most of you know, I miss church and friends more than anything. It's amazing how your faith can get you through so many of these things. You feel like you want to give up, and that there isn't anything that you can do about it. I know that I have every right to be weak, and I have every right to cry my little heart out whenever I want to because it isn't fair that this is happening to me, but you know what? I've had my little boo hoo party, and yes it does feel good to cry sometimes, but if I can keep showing others how much I love God throughout this whole ordeal, then I am happy. More than anything, I miss sitting back and singing old hymns. So today, my quotes are going to be some of my absolute favorite hymns that always make me smile and make me truly appreciate being the Christian that I am.

Love choo alll......
Lauren

P.S. I seriously just went through my iPod and these are my favorites. There are so many, hope you enjoy them!

"I am not skilled to understand
What God has willed, what God has planned
I only know at His right hand
Stands one who is my Savior

–Aaron Schust-"My Savior, My God"

"Turn your eyes upon Jesus, look full in His wonderful face, though the things of earth may grow strangely dim, in the light of His glory and grace...."
"O soul are you weary and troubled? No light in the darkness you see? There's light for a look at the Savior, and life more abundant and free..."
–Helen Lemmel-"Turn Your Eyes Upon Jesus"

"Into marvelous light I'm running, out of darkness out of shame, by the cross you are the truth you are the life you are the way... my dead heart now is beating, my deepest stains now clean, your breath fills up my lungs, now I'm free, now I'm free....sin has lost its power, death has lost its sting, from the grave you've risen victoriously....LIFT MY HANDS AND SPIN AROUND, SEE THE LIGHT THAT I HAVE FOUNDDDDDDDDDDD...
–Charlie Hall-"Marvelous Light"

"When peace like a river, attendeth my way, when sorrows like sea billows roll, whatever my lot Thou has taught me to say, it is well, it is well with my soul.
–Horatio Spafford-"It Is Well With My Soul"

"I am weak but you are strong, Jesus keep me from all wrong; I'll be satisfied as long as I walk, let me walk close to thee. Thru this world of toils and snares, if I falter Lord who cares? Who with me my burden shares? None but the dear Lord, none but Thee..."
–Songwriter Unknown-"Just a Closer Walk With Thee"

"Take my life and let it be, consecrated Lord to thee. Take my hands and let them move, at the impulse of Your Love..Take my feet and let them be swift and beautiful for thee. Take my voice and let me sing always, for my King. Take my silver and my gold, not a mite would I withhold. Take my moments and my days, let them flow in ceaseless praise. Take my well and make it thine, it shall be no longer mine....take my heart it is thine own, it shall be thy royal throne....take my life, all of me, here am I, all to thee...."
–Frances Havergal-"Take My Life and Let it Be"

"I will dance, I will sing to be mad for my King, nothing Lord is hindering this passion in my soul....and I'll become even more undignified than this, thought some may say it's foolishness.... leave my pride by my side!!"
–Matt Redman-"Undignified (I Will Dance, I Will Sing)"

"There is so much more to life than a pretty face and the perfect relationship. It's about loving God and sharing that love with others. Don't wait for it because it might not always be there. Be honest and just give your heart to God. He deserves it, not any random person."–Unknown

"and for all you've done, and yet to do...with every breath I'm praising you, desire of nations and every heart, you are alone are God.....you are the Lord, the famous one, famous one, great is your name in all the Earth....the heavens declare you are glorious, great is your fame beyond the Earth.
–Chris Tomlin-"Famous One"

"Your love has captured me, your grace has set me free, your life, the air I breathe....be glorified...."
–Chris Tomlin-"Be Glorified"

I totally didn't spell check this email and one of the side effects of my chemo is that my fingertips are numb so deal with it! Love you all!

• • • • • • • •

Sunday July 1, 2007

Subject: Quick update

Hey all!

Quick update, today was an awesome day. I feel better than I have in weeks and we made it to the Galleria for three hours! I finally started to get tired after lots of shopping. Mom, Dad and Eric did an awesome job of pushing me around in my new wheelchair. I had some guy buffer my nails and I didn't have the heart to tell him that I couldn't feel a thing because my finger tips are still numb from the chemo.

Anyways, that's my update for today! My appetite has come back full force (way excited about that), Keith Urban is on Tuesday, so pray for the trip up there to Austin (hopefully we can leave tomorrow) and then all of my procedures on Thursday, and then home on Friday or Saturday! Ya'll better be ready to see me! I love you all so much and I can't wait to see everyone! Keep the emails coming, I love hearing from everyone!

Love choo all
Lauren

"There is only one way to happiness, and that is to cease worrying about things that are beyond our will."–David Elkind

• • • • • • • •

Wednesday July 4, 2007

Subject: KEITH URBAN!!!!

Tell you what. God is pretty cool. You are all going to love this email I guarantee it. Get ready.

So, we made it to Austin great. Had a great car ride, didn't get sick, rained some, but we were good. Everyone knows why were going to Austin by now (other of course than to see my wonderful aunt, uncle and cousin) was because we had tickets to see Keith Urban. People amaze me, because within the past few weeks, people I don't even know have pulled strings to get me backstage passes, the whole nine yards. We ended up getting the backstage passes, super excited to go to the concert. We are ready.

Here's where the problem kind of started. The medicine that I am taking absolutely refuses to let me sleep. I literally lie in bed and just cannot sleep, my body rests but nothing else does. I don't sleep. Well, as of yesterday night, I hadn't slept in three days. The rain in Austin has started to make me sick (sore throat, you know the drill), which is not good. So, Tuesday morning, I'm feeling ok, kind of puny, blah. We needed to be at the concert by 5:45 in order to get my passes (we had two). We get in the car to go, and it just hit me. I was not going to make this backstage deal. My heart was beating irregular and I was just really short of breath. After about ten minutes of sitting in the car, I decided you know what, let my dad and my brother go, I'm going to go inside and rest. I love Keith Urban, but to me seeing the full concert was worth it more so than waiting four more hours for the actual concert and feeling awful. (The concert started at 7:30, had an opening act...so he wouldn't go onstage until like 8:45 anyways.)

I tell you what; this is where it gets super cool. I know that my dad and brother were totally bummed that I didn't get to meet Keith Urban, but I told them to do it for me, don't let this opportunity go to waste. They ended up having to stand in the rain, go through a lot of drama actually getting the tickets, something I just couldn't handle at this point because I felt so puny. They got in, and my dad is constantly calling saying, "everyone have their phones ready!" Of course you know I'm freaking out thinking, ya Keith Urban, call me?! KEITH URBAN CALLED ME FROM MY DAD'S PHONE! I TALKED TO KEITH URBAN!!! CAN YOU FRIGGIN' BELIEVE IT?!?!!?!??! I tell you what, poor guy. I'm screaming into the phone, I have no idea what was said, ok I lie he said he wished I was there, asked how I was feeling. Unbelievable. Even said he would dedicate a song to me. My dad said that he went up to Keith and said, "my daughter Lauren, she was supposed to be here but wasn't able to make it, she's sick." and Keith said "Lauren? Lime green? I know about her!" Then they tell my dad to hold on because they had something for me. I now am the proud owner of a lime green VIP concert pass that gets me backstage to any Keith Urban concert for the next two years!. So I talked to Keith Urban! And I will meet him! (It gets better.)

We made it to the concert, and God works in awesome ways, because we pulled right up to the front, no rain, no problems, made it to our seats just in time (which were awesome seats by the way) and enjoyed the whole concert. Stayed until the third song of the encore.

Here's where it gets kind of rough, but where I am truly thankful for what God gives me. I had a horrible night when we got home, just not being able to breathe, not being able to sleep. It's gotten to the point where I can't walk, like I almost have an anxiety attack by walking two feet. Amazing how much energy I have lost through this whole process. I am so truly thankful for the amazing support and love that my family has for me though. My father (those who know him, prepare yourself) *cuddled* up with me, read me bedtime stories about Bambi, rubbed my back for hours on end while I sit there crying because I am so homesick and I want to sleep more than anything. Who could ask for a better dad? My mom is amazing, she prays with me every night, along with my brother and dad, and I can't even begin to explain the undeniable love and faith that I have in my family. My aunt Denise too, she sat there and helped get lullabies together and rubbed my forehead just helping me fall asleep. I love them so much, and I thank God every single minute for everything that they do for me. My family that is at home, you know who you are, and I can't do this without you.

So, it gets better I promise. Today I've had a rough day just with crying and being a babbling brook about everything, and we get in the car to leave for Austin and I'm just upset and homesick. My mom asked me if I wanted my cell phone. I flip it open and realize I have just missed a private phone call. Two minutes later I have a voice mail. It's Keith Urban! He called *my cell phone*. I'm still in shock. If you don't believe me, I swear on my life I'll let you listen to it as soon as we get home. I missed the call but I don't even care because now I have a voice mail from Keith Urban on my phone. He loves me, has my phone number.....mmmmmmm. (Sean got worried, said he would do some Urban hunting if he had to.) Anyways, he thanked me for being a fan, told me people are praying for me, people love me, he met my dad and brother, hoped I felt better, said I'm checking my email, have your phone number in front of me. Unbelievable.

So, that's the Keith Urban update. If anyone of you don't own his cd's, tell me and I will gladly share with you. You need this man in your life he's awesome. I'm going to leave you with some Keith Urban song lyrics (go figure). So much has happened the past few days and I'm sure I've forgotten stuff. Tomorrow is a big procedure day but you all know that. Pray that everything works out this weekend and I'm able to come home. I'll see you all soon! I love choo all!

Lauren

"Oh now there's a place, for you and me, where we can dream as big as the sky, I know it's hard to see it now but baby someday we're gonna flyyyyyyyyyy.....This road we're on, you know it might be long, but my faith is strong, and that's all that really matters.... some day baby you and I going to be the ones, good luck's gonna shine, so hold on we're headed for a better life........."
–Songwriter: Richard Marx; Performed by Keith Urban-"Better Life"

When the sun is hard to find
When it's rainin' in your eyes
When the shadows block those pretty little blue skies living inside you
I'll find a way to shine"
–Songwriter Monty Powell; Performed by Keith Urban-"Shine"

• • • • • • •

Friday July 6, 2007

Subject: I'm HOME

Ahhh........I am HOME.

I love Corpus Christi. I love the Corpus Christi trees, the Corpus Christi birds, the Corpus Christi H-E-B, the Corpus Christi smell, the Corpus Christi people. I am absolutely thrilled to be home.

Today was a great day. I loved everything about it. We left Houston around 10, got to Corpus around 2:30 and I have felt great today. I am just so absolutely thrilled to be home. Our house is decorated in lime green and orange, I have an amazing bedroom set up by everyone, welcome home signs, I am so happy!

I have to go back to MD Anderson on July 17, so we have a little break. We won't know much until then as far as scans and everything else. We do know that I still have 2% of those blast cells in my bone marrow, but none of my results had really come in by yesterday and the doctor gave us the ok to come home, so here we are.

Thank you so much to everyone who has supported me throughout this whole process. We still have a long road ahead of us, but it's going to be just fine. Put your faith in God and He will take care of everything. These things are happening for a reason, and the change in myself is unbelievable. I know I have said it before, but it's amazing how many things we take for granted every day in life. The blueness of the sky, the greenness (is that a word?!) of the grass. The beauty of everyday life is something that should never be passed by.

I thank God every single day for this situation. Of course, it sucks that I have cancer, but to me, the way that it has brought my family closer to not only each other but God Himself amazes me. I'm not in any way saying that cancer is what has brought everyone together, but in my eyes, the process of everything has shown other people that through the bad, God is still numero uno. I can't even begin to *explain* the outpouring of love and excitement that I have every single time I think about what He has done for me.

It's late; I didn't bother to read through this email twice so forgive the spelling mistakes if there are any. Love choo alll!

Lauren

"Many people go from one thing to another searching for happiness, but with each new venture they find themselves more confused and less happy until they discover that what they are searching for is inside themselves and what will make them happy is sharing their real selves with the ones they love,"–Unknown

"The greater the obstacle the more glory in overcoming it." –Moliere

• • • • • • • •

Tuesday July 10, 2007

Subject: Give the girl a break already!

Ugh.

So, Friday and Saturday were good days. Friday was awesome, I felt better than I have in a long time, got to hang out with family, Saturday was good too other than being super tired. Sunday, what a Sunday.

I woke up, went to church (which was so super awesome I love it), but ended up going home right after because I got really really tired. I slept a lot of the day on Sunday, and then got to hang out with my girlfriends (who are all awesome and wore matching bandanas when they came over).

Here's where the problem starts. I have been having this issue with pain in my back, shoulders, arms, neck and chest and having a hard time breathing. Saturday night was rough, but I was able to handle the pain to a point. Sunday night, no can do. I have a high pain tolerance, and it got to the point where I just couldn't do it anymore. My skin is really sensitive to the touch, and I just felt like something wasn't right. My heart rate was in the 120's (it's usually in the 80's) and it just felt like my heart was beating out of my chest. Mom and Dad decided to go ahead and take me to the hospital, which was definitely the right decision. We got to the hospital, and I still felt like I couldn't breathe, but we were able to get into a room right away and they gave me a lot of morphine, which made things much better. We got to the hospital around 10:30 pm, and my heart rate was super high, so throughout the night they tried to get my heart rate down, but it never did go down, just fluctuated between 120 and 140 all night. Around 4:30 am I was admitted to the hospital and I've been here ever since.

Yesterday was a rough day just because once again I didn't sleep Sunday night, and a lot of people wanted to come and visit on Monday, which is fine, but it got to the point where I had to tell people to leave. I felt super bad about it, but I needed to sleep. I think I got maybe a couple of hours in and felt a little bit better. Later that night, I was getting medicine put into my IV and I noticed that it was really painful, just burning and uncomfortable. Some of you have seen the bruise that I have on my right arm (where the IV was). The entire top of it turned red and ended up getting super swollen. Not fun.

I told the nurse I needed a new IV, that I didn't want to use that one anymore because it hurt, so they sent a girl in to start my new IV, and I really don't think she knew what she was doing. I have a vein that I know I have had an IV in before and I kept telling her, put it in that vein I promise it will work, and she tried another vein, poked around for a while, and then decided she didn't want to poke me anymore so she was going to let my nurse put the IV in. So, my nurse came in and started my IV, no problem.

Today I find out I have to have a blood transfusion and a breathing treatment. The transfusion is because I'm anemic, and the breathing treatment is because I have a really bad cough, not good. In fact as we speak, I'm getting my transfusion, neat huh? Anyways, we think that my central line has a leak in it, wonderful. Hear the sarcasm in my voice? We started the transfusion in my central line, and then my dad was like, uhh, you're bleeding. Sure enough, the blood that I was getting was leaking out of the line, we tried flushing the line and that leaked out as well. So I still ended up having to get another IV because the second one they put in was too small. So right now I'm looking at my hand and I have an IV site in my vein below my thumb and then in the big vein that's in the middle of my hand. Bummer. Hopefully I get to go home tomorrow, but now my doctor just told me that they can replace my central line here in Corpus, so, who knows when I will get to leave this place. It's nice having parents that work here though. I like knowing that I am in the best hospital here in Corpus!

So, that is the latest. I'm kind of bummed about being in the hospital, but it's like I told my parents, I would rather be here and them figure out why I am in so much pain and get good pain medicine than go home and be miserable because I'm in pain. Kudos to my parents and family for sticking it out with me, Lord knows I can't do it without them.

Love choo all..........
Lauren

p.s....sorry no spell check!

"He reached down from on high and took hold of me; he drew me out of deep waters. He rescued me from my powerful enemy, from my foes, who were too strong for me. They confronted me in the day of my disaster, but the Lord was my support. He brought me out into a spacious place; he rescued me because he delighted in me." Psalm 18:16-19 (NIV)

• • • • • • • •

Thursday July 12, 2007

Subject: Once again, I'm home!

It feels good to be in my own bed.

It's been an interesting weekend. I do apologize for being just a bit bitter in my last email. I was medicated, in pain, and slightly ticked off. I'm all better now.

I was discharged from the hospital yesterday around 9 pm, and I feel a million times better after my blood transfusion. I was able to sleep through the night, which was great. Aunt Ann and Memaw were excellent nurses today. We went to the cancer center and had fun trying on different wigs. It was either get three used wigs for free or one brand new one. Believe me, we had the time of our lives trying on the old wigs. I swear, they were straight from 1970! Pretty hideous, but I found a wig! And it looks pretty darn good!

We also went shopping, back to the hospital to show off the wig, and back home. It's been a fabulous day! As far as my pain goes, I'm doing a lot better, but I'm still in a pretty significant amount of pain. For some weird reason, I'm just super sensitive to touch in my back and neck. My new catheter is kind of cool, you can actually see it through my neck. Gross.

Anyways, I don't really have much else to say. I hope ya'll still read my emails and I hope ya'll are still interested in learning about what is going on. This battle is definitely not over yet!

I know I've mentioned it, but I never remember what I write in old emails, but we are leaving for Houston again on Monday, the 16th for my second round of chemo. Oh ya, they also think that another possibility for the hole in my catheter was the actual chemo itself, didn't think about that! And I also went to the restaurant where I used to work. It was so good to see all of my co-workers! They were all so supportive and awesome the whole time we were there! Same with family and friends, ya'll are awesome! I hope the emails aren't getting old, or boring, I try to keep them interesting!

love choo all......
Lauren

"Our ultimate aim in life is not be healthy, wealthy, prosperous, or problem free, our ultimate aim in life is to bring glory to God."–Unknown

"The natural healing force within each one of us is the greatest force in getting well."–Hippocrates

"Sometimes we are overwhelmed with the obstacles we are given in our lives, and we ask 'why me?' And often, when the answers elude us, we believe that the trials through which we suffer are unfair and harsh. But there ARE answers, even though we may not recognize them. In this world, we are all connected, and there is a reason for whatever happens. We must remain strong in the face of adversity and meet the challenges one day at a time. And as time heals us, both body and soul, we may come to understand the meaning of our trials or recognize the good that came from them. We may take pride in knowing that we made it through them, and as a result are much stronger than we were before. When we are going through a difficult time in life, we must accept what has happened and know that things will get better."–Unknown

• • • • • • •

Tuesday July 17, 2007

Subject: So we are back in Houston...

Ok, so good news and bad news!

We will get the good news out first. I'm in REMISSION! Yay! I responded really well to the chemo and because my bone marrow is below five percent, it's considered remission. More good news, if all goes well and I don't have any delays, the chemo will only last about 5 1/2 to 6 1/2 months, which is way shorter than I thought.

The bad news? Although I'm super excited about remission, I'm really bummed this week. I was supposed to be well and be a sponsor for the youth camp Zephyr. Those who know me know that I live for times like this because it is such a good opportunity to reach out to teenagers about God and I'm really really bummed that I'm not able to be there. There are certain people that are going this year that are going for the last time, and I really wanted to go, but obviously I'm not there. So, I'm kind of bummed.

Here's the lowdown on the chemo. The first round is two months, at the end of that I have one more bone marrow aspiration. That is consolidation 1. Consolidation 2 is a month and a half, consolidation 3a is about a month, and same with 3b. Then I hit maintenance, which is just less medicine, but not quite as bad. They said that I should feel a lot better somewhere between consolidation 3b and maintenance.

I can't start chemo until Thursday because I'm getting over a sinus infection. The doctor put me on some new antibiotic to get rid of my cough, but the chemo that I am taking on Thursday is *eight* hours long. Ugh.

Anyways, that is the latest. I'm sorry I have no quotes today, my quote book is very far away from me in the hotel room and I'm tired and don't feel like getting up. I love choo all!

Lauren

• • • • • • • •

Wednesday July 18, 2007

Subject: Yup, two in a row!

You know what? I figure if I can't be at camp helping out teenagers, maybe I can help others out with my emails. I know I just sent an email yesterday, but something is telling me that I need to write this email, that someone needs to read it.

I just finished reading this book that Sean bought me. It's the Chicken Soup for Survivors (those who know me well know I love the Chicken Soup series and I own tons of them). The entire book is about people who have survived cancer and lived to tell their stories. It really got me thinking, you know, I'm *blessed* to have the type of cancer I have. I'm *blessed* to have the support system that I have. I'm *blessed* to live in Texas and only be four hours away from MD Anderson Cancer Center. I'm *blessed* to have a mom who is a nurse and can spot things others might not. I'm *blessed* that I know who God is, and I see what He can do.

While reading this book, the majority of the people looked at cancer as a death sentence. The minute they found out their diagnosis, they immediately asked, "what's my survival rate?" I thought to myself, I never even asked that question. Turns out my survival rate for the type of cancer I have has a 95% success rate with early treatment, and I'm already in remission. I mean, really, how much greater can God get?

I really started to think about everything, and as I was reading this book, a lot of these people automatically looked at cancer as a death sentence. They automatically think, cancer is going to kill me and there's nothing I can do about it. But they begin to think about things, and they put things into perspective, and they slowly realize that God is the most important thing and so much of the healing process lies within the attitude of the person who has cancer and the attitude of the people around them. If the people around you become depressed and down, how in the world is the person who is sick supposed to stay motivated?

Although I am in remission, it's hard to think about the next six months and how I will get through it. There will be bad days, guaranteed, and I face a lot of giants in the near future. I can choose to be scared, which of course, I am, and I can choose to fight it with all I've got, which I will. Although I am scared about it all, I know I will get through it, there is no doubt in my mind what the outcome will be. I will rely on my faith, and I know who will get me through this. I found a great quote.

"Fear knocked at the door. Faith answered it....no one was there."
–Anonymous

So, you have to remember how important God is in your life. There is no denying it, and those who don't realize it better open up their eyes because eventually, you will come to a point where you come face to face with Him and have to make a decision. You want others to see God through you, and you can't do that if you are depressed all the time. These last few days I've had a rough time thinking about the next six months, but I decided today that I need to just take things day by day and keep prayin'. I truly truly believe in the power of prayer, and I really think that when people just close their eyes and start talking to God it will honestly make you feel so much better, at least I know it makes me feel better. There is nothing greater than being in a room with people praying, and knowing that these people are being broken by God and He will lead them in the right direction to be healed.

You have the option. It's right in front of you, and all you have to do is take it. You need to count your blessings, not your worries. Don't try to fight it, and don't try to talk yourself into thinking, "oh, if I tithe every week, if I pray every so often, if I witness to one person a month......" because eventually those thoughts will turn into, "well, God will forgive me for that drink I drank, God will forgive me for saying that cuss word, God will forgive me doing those things that I shouldn't be doing." Yes, God will forgive you, but you *cannot* keep saying, "God will forgive me every time, so it's ok if I keep doing it." Like I said, it's totally within your reach. The walk of faith is not easy; I believe it's harder for people who do believe than those who don't believe. The outcome is so rewarding though. You just have to *believe* in Him, and *trust* in him, and *love* Him, because He loved you enough to give His son. I know everyone has heard that so many times, but think about how much you love your children, those who have them. You know you would do anything for them......but would you let them hang on a cross with nails in his or her hands and feet, crown of thorns, and know they would die?

Seriously think about it. It just popped into my mind how amazing everything is. Just think about it.

I know that I am young, and people keep telling me that I inspire them. I don't. It's flattering to hear people tell me that, but it's not me. I don't inspire you, it's God working *through* me. It's not me you see, it's God. Not me.

On a medical note, we figured out why I had so much pain in the hospital. When I was getting my chemotherapy, it would suppress my bone marrow, killing off my good cells. Well, when I had the break from the chemo, my bone marrow went into overdrive making good cells and apparently that was what caused all my pain. Interesting huh? Oh ya, my new central line? Works like a charm. I love it, and the people at MD Anderson better like it too because I don't want any more put in! Pray for my long day tomorrow, and pray that we can figure out some kind of schedule so I can be in Corpus for the majority of it. And that the feeling in my fingers and toes will come back because I'm tired of them being numb! And that I will stop being so gosh darn shaky. Ok

I'm done. I have quotes for you today, so I hope that excites some of you.

Love choo all....
Lauren

"In his heart a man plans his course, but the Lord determines his steps." Proverbs 16:9 (NIV)

"'But I will restore you to health and heal your wounds', declares the Lord". Jeremiah 30:17 (NIV)

"For only God can know these things....the day, the hour, the time, but on this day I am alive and all the world is mine."–Jill Warren

"Happiness isn't about what happens to us, it's about how we perceive what happens to us. It's the knack of finding a positive for every negative, and viewing a setback as a challenge. If we can just stop wishing for what we don't have, and start enjoying what we do have, our lives can be richer, more fulfilled, and happier. The time to be happy is NOW."–Lynn Peters

"If you accept defeat, that's what you are going to get."–Unknown

stick with me...one more quote....read every word of it.

"The past is gone, but NOW is forever. The future does not lie in our hands, but the future lies in the hands of the present. Go out and grasp the seconds of the day as if you only had that day to live. Experience and enjoy the moments of your life. We only have one life to live, so live it like a champion. Everyone was put here for a purpose, so let that purpose rise up about and show everyone what you're made of. I'm not telling you how you should live, but how you should feel when you look back on the memories of a once-upon life of yours. Don't regret things later. If you feel it is right, do it. It's your life and nobody else's. Make decisions that please you. Let nobody put you down. Don't live in anybody's shadow or dreams. If you do have a dream, act on it and it will probably come true."–Chicken Soup for the Survivors Soul-Jack Canfield

• • • • • • • •

Tuesday, July 21, 2007

Subject: Starting to get frustrated....

I am in a prison.....and that prison is my bedroom.

It's very hard for me to be told I can't do things, that I can't see my friends, that I can't pet my dog or see my kittens....grrr. I shock myself when I look in the mirror because I don't look like myself. I look at pictures of me and my friends and it seems like such a long time ago, and it's very frustrating to think that I am going to completely miss out on at least a year of growing up with my friends. Most of them will graduate in May and move on to other cities. I just want to hang out with my friends!!!

It amazes me how cancer completely transforms your life. I never imagined that I could deal with everything I have to deal with, but I have no choice. I refuse to just wither up and watch cancer take over. In case you didn't know, I have plans. And I have every intention of following through with my plans, so cancer, step aside, and get out of my way.

Sorry, that was my little letter to lymphoma. Had to get it out.

I've been stuck in bed since last Thursday. I had my lumbar puncture on Friday. I've been fortunate enough not to have any spinal headaches (a pretty big side effect) in my previous punctures. On Sunday, I started to walk around and noticed I had a terrible headache and lots of back pain. We figured it was a spinal headache on Monday when we went to the cancer center. I tell you what, spinal headaches really suck. Feels like your head is going to explode at any minute. You can't really stand up without being super unbalanced and feeling sick. The only way to fix it is lots of bed rest and lots of fluids.

I'm supposed to have two more lumbar punctures within the next two weeks and chemo along with those. I feel really comfortable in the cancer center here in Corpus, everyone is so nice and I really like the atmosphere.

Anywho, that's the latest update! Sorry I didn't spell check I'm being lazy!

love choo allllllllllllllllllllllllllll
Lauren

• • • • • • • •

Wednesday July 25, 2007

Subject: Oh Corpus Christi, how I miss thee....

Apparently, you crazy people out there like my emails, so I shall keep writing them.

The first four days of chemo went pretty well, but one of the bad side effects of it is that the medicine drops my blood counts by a lot. For example, on Saturday, my white blood cell count was 3.79, on Tuesday it was 1.72. Apparently when you get down to 1.0 your risk for infection increases a lot (at least that is how I understand it). So, bummer there. And I still have a little bit of a cough, but it is so much better than it was. We figured that we would only have to be in Houston for about a week, at least that is kind of what the doctors led us to believe.

So, when we went to the doctor yesterday, she tells us that we are scheduled for chemo in Houston on Thursday through Sunday. Umm....hello....Corpus Christi? So, the doctor in Houston (Dr. Thomas) agrees that we can do the chemo in Corpus, but before we leave Houston she wanted to talk to the oncologist here in Corpus and make sure that I could get the medicine here. Guess what, the doctor is out of town. So, Dr. Manalo (CC) doesn't get the orders until today. They are still trying to work things out so the big prayer request at this point is that they will give me the chemo here in Corpus. Otherwise, we drive to Houston in the morning for four more days of boringness.

The downside to having the chemo here in Corpus is that I will have to be admitted the hospital all four days of chemo. Bummer, but hey, I would be in Corpus and be able to have visits from my super cool friends.

I got to go to church tonight! I loved it. It was so awesome to see everyone and all my friends. It felt great to be in an environment with normal, smiling happy people (not that my family and friends aren't, but you know). I got to see the camp pictures, and catch up with people. Super awesome

Anyways, that's the latest update. Really hoping that we can get the chemo done here in Corpus and that the cough will go away. I still have numbness in my hands and feet.

I'm really not looking forward to the next six months, because for some reason or another, I have a feeling that I'm truly going to be tested. I know that it is not going to be easy in any way, and I dread it. But like I have said a million times, without the support of my family and friends there is no way I could get through it. I really am beginning to struggle with it, as far as becoming more irritable, short with people, etc. I'm frustrated with myself, because I see that I'm doing it. Grrrr. That's all.

That's all I've got for now....let you know whenever I know something.

Love choo all...........
Lauren

"Our lives are made up of a million moments, spent in a million different ways. Some are spent searching for love, peace, and harmony. Others are spent surviving day to day. But there is no greater moment than when we find that life-with all its joys and sorrows-is meant to be lived one day at a time. It's in this knowledge that we discover the most wonderful truth of all. Whether we live in a forty-room mansion, surrounded by servants and wealth, or find it a struggle to manage the rent month to month, we have it within our power to be fully satisfied and live a life with true meaning. One day at a time-we have that ability, through cherishing each moment and rejoicing in each dream. We can experience each day anew, and with this fresh start we have what it takes to make all of our dreams come true. Each day is new, and living one day at a time enables us to truly enjoy life and live it to the fullest."–Unknown

• • • • • • • •

Sunday July 29, 2007

Subject: Update!

Hola friends!!

Well, I was discharged from the hospital today (yay!). I tell you what, I am so very grateful for the treatment that MD Anderson gives me, but nothing can compare to being home. The nurses that took care of me here in Corpus were so awesome and encouraging every day. I stayed on the oncology floor at the hospital, and the first night that I was there my nurse told me that there were no restrictions on visiting hours, to have my friends come and go as they please. At one point we thought we were in trouble for laughing too loud, but it turns out all the nurses loved it and encouraged us to keep on. They were so good to us, and I'm super thankful for them. It was so great to see my friends.... Molly and Dominique came to visit me the first night I was there. Because I was on neutropenic (who knows if that is spelled right) precautions, people who visited had to wear masks around me, I couldn't have fresh flowers, stuff like that. So it was a real laugh to see Molly and Dom in those masks and gloves, especially because they both looked like dinosaurs. If I had pictures, I would so send them.

They decided to go ahead and give me a blood transfusion the first night that I was there because my counts were super low. The transfusion worked and got my white blood cell count up to 4.9 (It was 1.4). Chemo was super fast, only took about an hour. The doctor prescribed me a new medicine that is supposed to help with the numbness in my fingers and toes, so hopefully that will work out. I've done so much reading the past few days. My friend Kylee bought me "The Sisterhood of the Traveling Pants" for my birthday, and I finally read it and then made my mom go buy the sequels to it, and I read those too.

I'm scheduled for chemo here in Corpus at least through Thursday, so I know I will be in Corpus till Thursday. I'm not sure when we go to Houston again though. I'm not too sure that I like the way they do the lumbar punctures here in Corpus, that was the one thing I was kind of disappointed in. In Houston, they make you sit on the edge of the bed and lean over the little tray table deally bopper thing a majig and they get into your spine that way. The doctor here in Corpus made me lay flat on my side and curl my legs up. The only good thing about it was that it was over in less than 5 minutes, but now my back still hurts.

I'm hoping that this two month consolidation will go by quickly. This is supposed to be one of the more aggressive ones. We are two weeks in, so six weeks to go!!

With that said, thanks for all the prayers, support and love. Right back at ya folks.

Love choo allll..........
Lauren

"God has equipped you ahead of time to face every trial-and He is with you no matter what."–Joel Osteen

"Each of us may be sure that if God sends us on stony paths, He will provide us with strong shoes, and He will not send us out on any journey for which He does not prepare us well."–Alexander Maclaren

"Keep your face towards the sunshine and you can't see the shadows."–Helen Keller

"Sometimes it seems like we can't go on a moment longer. Our own strength is all used up, and we feel as though we are falling into pieces. Life is just too much for us to handle. But it's ok to feel like that; you don't have to be strong all the time. Times like that you just have to let go - and allow God the chance to take over. His strength never fails."–Unknown

• • • • • • • •

Saturday August 4, 2007

Subject: Update.

Ok, this is the THIRD time I have tried to write this update!! It keeps getting erased!!!

Two days ago I woke up in the emergency room. Apparently my mom went into my room and I wasn't responding at all. She called 911, a bunch of firemen came into my room, took me away on the ambulance, and took me to the hospital. I remember none of this. Weird huh? They said it was just confusion or something like that.

Anyways, I'm fine now. I still have a really bad headache, my back hurts a lot, and I noticed that I'm starting to bruise a lot easier. Oh well. It will all be over within a few months. They held off my lumbar puncture and one of my chemos till Tuesday (THANK JESUS). I also have an appointment with my academic advisor on Monday to see if there are any classes I can take online. I want to graduate at some point! Hopefully there is something, kind of hard to take a communication class online.

I'm still locked up in my house, trying to find things to do. So, if you have any ideas, send them my way. Hope you are all doing well!

Love choo alll.....
Lauren

P.S. You should all see my latest hairstyle. It's pretty funny....
pigtails.

• • • • • • • •

Wednesday August 8, 2007

Subject: When it rains....

.....it pours.

Here I am at my home-away-from-home, good ole Houston, Texas. Trust me, I would much rather be in the good ole C squared. A bunch of people have been asking how I am, so I'm going to tell you, whoopeeee.

I'm not doing so well. Ever since my last lumbar puncture, I have had terrible headaches. I can't stand up for more than five minutes without getting completely nauseated, so I'm laying down all the time. I haven't been able to get chemo for about a week because my counts are super, super low. My white blood cells are at 0.5 (normal range is 4.6-10) and my platelets are 40,000 (normal range is 150,000-400,000). Ya, I'm pretty puny right now.

People have been asking about the details of my illness, so here ya go. Initially I was diagnosed with lymphoma because the cancer started in my lymph nodes. When we found out the cancer was also in my blood, it then became leukemia. Leukemia is basically cancer of the blood. The type that I have (ALL) has a good prognosis with prolonged treatment. I have to go through 5 phases of chemo, and then once that's finished, I have two years of maintenance, which is like chemo once a month and lumbar punctures every three months. I have to keep getting the lumbar punctures because the type of cancer that I have is known to relapse in the spine, so yay for me, more needles in my back. The 5 phases of chemo will take about 6 months or so, just depending on my counts and whether or not we have to take breaks in between the phases. I am in remission, which means that the cancer is no longer spreading and is under control. I still have to have treatment though to kill off all those bad guys, but unfortunately, it kills off the good guys too, which is why I never feel good.

Yesterday I was supposed to get chemo and a lumbar puncture, but seeing that my counts were as low as they were, Dr. Manalo decided it would be best to go ahead and give me a platelet transfusion and a blood transfusion. Because I am on a scheduled treatment plan (protocol), Dr. Manalo calls my doctor in Houston, Dr. Thomas, a lot to make sure we are staying on track. I completely trust my nurses and doctors in Corpus, and I trust my doctors in Houston. So, after a horrible night last night (had awful back pain again due to the bone marrow working overtime – seriously, it was a 10 out of 10 on the pain scale), Dr. Thomas' nurse calls us today and said that we had to be in Houston tomorrow morning because Dr. Thomas wants to see me for herself. Which is fine, but a bummer.

So, mom, dad and me pack it up and drive to Houston. Thank God for parents because they make the trip easy by making things easy for me. I promise one day I will pay it all back when I can move freely with no pain!

I'm also bummed because I really wanted to go to the benefit BBQ on Saturday just to say thanks to everyone. I can't begin to tell you how much I appreciate everything that everyone has done to help us out, it's unbelievable. I promise to give ya'll an update within the next couple of days to let you know how things are going here in H-town, my favorite city in the world (gag me).

Love choo allllllllll
Lauren

P.s. we just realized that we have no power cord for my computer and my computer is about to die. Yup, it's pouring.

"He forgives all my sins and heals all my diseases." Psalm 103:3 (NIV)

"How refreshing to know You don't need me

61

How amazing to find that You want me
So I'll stand on Your truth, and I'll fight with Your strength
Until you bring the victory, by the power of Christ in me"
–Songwriter: Mark Hall; Performed by Casting Crowns-"In Me"

• • • • • • • •

Sunday August 12, 2007

Subject: Update from the cancer girl!

Holaaaaaaa mis amigos-----

The barbeque was a huge success!! It is amazing to see that that many people care, and that many people show their support. Makes me feel super special!

As far as my health is going, I'm ok. As shallow as it sounds, I have a lot of trouble with the physical effects of the chemo more so than the sickness that comes with it. Ya it sucks to be sick all the time, but I can just sleep through it. When I wake up, there is no changing how I look. It's hard to lose my hair (which is still falling out by the way, I'll hang on to every last bit!), and the mouthwash that I have to use stains my teeth. Good thing I had some pretty white ones to begin with! It makes you gain weight, and makes you feel like you are a super old woman with arthritis or something. You can't bend over to pick anything up, your hands start to hurt, and you aren't able to go out and do the things that you want to do.

That's the other super frustrating thing about having such low counts; I'm not able to really hang out with my friends. I really believe that laughter and friendship is a huge part of my healing process, so it's hard when I can't have that. It's ok though, I just have to look forward to the times that I can spend with them.

My headaches have gotten a lot better. Oh ya, we were able to come home on Friday! I forgot that I haven't written an email in a while! Dr. Thomas prescribed me some magnesium pills and a pill called Flexeril that helps with muscle spasms, basically like a muscle relaxant. I had my lumbar puncture there in Houston on Thursday, and although I still have headaches, they are in no way as severe as they were. I also had two other chemos, Vincristine and Pegulated Asparagenase, or however you spell it. We call it asparagus. Those three chemo's put together knocked me down for a couple of days, but now my biggest problem is being achy and trying to work my muscles. Because I've been lying in bed so much, it seems like my leg and back muscles are starting to weaken.

So we go back Wednesday night and find out what the full plan is on Thursday. Keep in touch, I love to hear from you all!

love choo alllllllllll
Lauren

All these are super cheesy but I love them and they make me happy!

"Pain is inevitable: suffering is optional."–Haruki Murikami

"Do not spoil what you have by desiring what you have not." –Epicurus

"Experience is a hard teacher because she gives the test first, the lesson afterward."–Vernon Sanders Law

"I will be strong.
I will laugh.
I will cry.
I will win.

I FOUGHT.
I LAUGHED.
I CRIED.
We WON."–Anonymous

• • • • • • • •

Wednesday August 15, 2007

Subject: Another e-mail.

For some reason or another, I really felt like I had to write this email, right now at 2:26 in the AM. I totally should be sleeping but whatever.

Throughout this whole process, music really does take the edge off of things. (I think I might have mentioned this before, so forgive me if this is a repeat. I'll just blame it on the chemo brain so whatever!) Ok, back to seriousness. Music means so much to me, and just listening to certain songs kind of calms me down or makes things not as stressful. One of the big things that bugs me about this whole cancer deal is that I really haven't been able to make it to church. We tend to end up leaving Wednesday nights and staying through the weekend, or I'm feeling too puny to go.

Side note - I know for a fact that there are people within my own church that have cancer but still keep on trucking and make it every Sunday morning. YOU inspire ME.

Moving on, I miss church. I miss hanging out on Wednesday nights with everyone, playing a little ping pong or pool, or just chillin' out in the black light room. (church people know what I'm talking about!). I miss walking into the sanctuary and looking at the gorgeous stained glass, being amazed by our baptistry, just everything. I have gone to this church since I can remember, so obviously it means a lot to me and I miss it.

Ok, back to music. Bear with me, I promise. Someone will get something out of it. There is a Christian band called Casting Crowns, pretty popular I guess. Their music has inspired me so much, in so many ways I can't even begin to tell you. Anyways, I was laying here listening to some of their songs, and one song that I've listened to a gajabillion times, I think I've even quoted it in a previous email, really made me open my eyes. I'm going to include the lyrics for you, hopefully you see what I mean. This song comes out on the radio, so I'm sure some of you have heard it.

Chorus:
And I'll praise you in this storm and I will lift my hands
that you are who you are no matter where I am
and every tear I've cried you hold in your hand...
I will praise you in this storm

–Songwriter: Bernie Herms; Performed by Casting Crowns-"Praise You in this Storm"

So that's the song. Some of you may think, oh what's this crazy girl thinking, it's just a song. It's so much more than that. When I first got diagnosed, I can't even begin to tell you the things that ran through my mind. Knowing that I would never be the same, knowing that I was going to go through so much pain, and knowing how hard it would be on everyone. You don't know until you have to deal with it yourself. The song talks about God stepping in to save the day. Well, if He was God and wants good for all of His people then why would He pull something like this? In all honesty, that thought totally ran through my mind. You pray at night and say, "why in the world am I the one who has to deal with it?" It's because He *chose* you to do it. It also talks about not being able to find God, and in my own naive mind going to church was always my way of staying connected, kind of like a constant reminder of, ok Lauren, you need to do this, this and this and live your life a certain way. I've come to realize that it doesn't matter. Church or not, I can still praise God whenever I want to because He is always with me. That doesn't mean I'm saying to not go to church!! (oh geez, I hope I don't get into trouble for this one!)

Ok, so if ya'll are still with me, you rock! I don't know if any of that made sense, but it did to me. And it made me feel better, so there. We leave to Houston in about 16 hours or so. We know for sure that I am getting a lumbar puncture on Thursday at MD Anderson but we still don't know about the 4 day chemo cycle. My dad and Eric are staying here for this trip, so hopefully that goes well. Pray for my Memaw, she's having some doctor stuff done on Friday so we hope that goes well.

People keep telling me that I inspire them. Let me remind you once again, it's not me.

Everyone else inspires me so keep the emails coming. I love you all and I can't wait to have a huge party once this all over with. I think it's going to be a mask-burning party! (I have to wear a mask everywhere because of the cooties ya'll have).

I love choooo alllllllllllllllllll...........
Lauren

● ● ● ● ● ● ●

Friday August 24, 2007

Subject: And we are back in the game!

So, in my mind, I have this idea to write out this email as if it were an amusement park ride, because that's how it was pretty much all day yesterday. Or not, we will see how it works out.

We got home on Sunday and I was able to eat some of this awesome vegetable soup my dad made (it's like my favorite food ever). I've been having a lot of issues with nausea the last few days, so of course when you are nauseated, food is an issue. I haven't really been able to eat much of anything except the soup and some crackers. I don't think I have had a substantial meal since around Monday night, but it is all due to the nausea. Grrrrrrrrr.

So we leave for Houston on Wednesday, get to our hotel, and realize I don't have a contact case. So me and mom went on a scavenger hunt to try and find cases at CVS Pharmacy, no luck, so then we went to Walgreens (I just have to say, I truly love that store) and found everything we needed, plus some extra snacks for the hotel.

On Thursday, we got to MD Anderson around 8:00 am, got lab work done, and waited about 2.5 hours to get to our doctor's appointment. Once we finally get there, the doctor was concerned about a lot of different things and decided that it was probably best to admit me into the hospital. The problem was that the hospital was at full occupancy, no beds available. So, the plan was to send me off to the Emergency Room because all the tests that I needed to get done would go by a lot faster and I could just wait there for a bed. This is kind of where all the amusement park ride idea came to mind.

My first test they sent me off for was a Catscan. I've had one before, and I never remembered it being something terrible.

68

They have to inject you with this stuff called Iodine, which is some type of dye that goes into your body at a temperature of about 100 degrees. They can only inject it in certain places, like the mid section of your arm, because a machine is what injects it and tends to be kind of forceful, so you have to have a good IV site. Well, my lovely ER people knew this, and they set me up with an IV in my left arm (the other crappy thing is that they have to use a bigger needle than usual to get the Iodine through). Anyways, I'm set to go. We were told that the scan would last about 45 minutes or so, no biggie. Once we got up to the Scan Unit, it was like a huge traffic jam of stretchers. One was before me and one was behind me, so it was kind of like we are all in line to go get on this super cool ride, "The CatScan". They set us all up, and everyone around me seemed to have difficulty with their IV sites. So, three people go before me (they cut in line if you will), and I'm still sitting there, kind of just twiddling my thumbs, when the nurse comes up to me and asked "are you done with your catscan sweetie?" ummmmmm nooooo I'm waiting for you to do all this pre-stuff so I can be done. Sure enough, they had lost my file or something. The people that had come down with me to ride the ride were already coming out, big smiles on their faces, some looking slightly anxious, and I'm like, second to last. Usually I do pretty well with the majority of these things (including amusement park rides), but seeing the people's faces afterwards was just a little bit nerve-wracking. I've had this Iodine injection before, but I don't remember it being something terrible. Well, it was. They lay you on a table with your arms over your head. The reason why I kept thinking of it like a ride was because you lay there, and the little voice overhead keeps saying, "ok, breathe in.....hold it...... breathe". It's very automated. I think it's pretty funny. There are little signs everywhere saying don't look at the laser, and then the machine starts spinning around you, then slows down, like it's revving it's engine or something. Weird huh? Anyways, then they inject the Iodine into your arm and its awful! It goes in really fast, it's super hot, and it is like the worst feeling ever! It goes through your entire body really fast and takes over your entire body and you feel like you are going to pee on yourself, ok maybe that was too much info. Afterwards, I had some shortness of breath and got a little bit pale, but the good thing about your nurses losing you the first time is that after they realize they do so, they treat you like you are some VIP patient. By the time I left, they were all yelling that they missed me and to come back and see them.

So, then I went on some more rides, the chest x-ray adventure, ultrasound-go-round, blood transfusion, you get the picture. It was a long day overall. Final outcome? Turns out I have a tiny blood clot in my lung, called a Pulmonary Embolus. Pretty serious if we hadn't found out about it. The way they fix it is by giving me a shot every twelve hours for the next three months. I HATE SHOTS. Seriously, I'm a *huge* baby when it comes to stuff like that, they burn!

In the end, we are still at MD Anderson now, they say that hopefully I can be discharged tomorrow. At least that's the plan. We waited around in the ER for a room for nine hours, which is fine, got a room about 11:45 last night, and I'm sure we will be back in Houston till Tuesday.

Love choo alll..............
Lauren

• • • • • • •

Monday August 27, 2007

Subject: I'd like you to meet my white blood cells....

....since I have so few of them, I went ahead and named them Whitey, Nerdy, Rainbow, Star, Flip and Flop. That's about all that I have.

Although my counts are still super low, I'm feeling a lot better. We were able to shop around the other day, get some stuff done. The doctors went ahead and decided that it would be best to overlap my chemo. So I start a four day regimen today, along with the IV antibiotics. Then on Thursday, they are going to slam me with 3 different chemos and the antibiotics. Ouch. Because of everything that has been going on with the blood clot, Dr. Thomas doesn't want me to leave Houston until she sees us on Tuesday. Bummer! We have already been here since last Thursday, and there is only so much you can do in a hotel room. Good thing me and my mom are easily entertained by our computers.

The good news is, I'm almost done! Here is the breakdown for the next few months, give or take, I think.

Consolidation 2- I get chemo every ten days for 4 weeks and then I get a two week break.
Consolidation 3a is 29 days long and I get chemo on days 1, 4, 8 and 15.
Consolidation 3b is four days of chemo for two weeks, and then once a week for two weeks.

Then I'm done! NO MORE CHEMO! At least for a while. I'll still have chemo once I'm in maintenance, but not near as much as I am now. I know it's all kind of confusing, but I try to understand it all.

I'm still in good spirits, much better than I have been. I can't really go out and do things because of my counts being so low, but I'm trying to find things to do here. That's all folks!!

Love choo allllllllllllllllllllllll..........
Lauren

"Your imagination is your preview of life's coming attractions."-Albert Einstein

"The difference between a successful person and others is not a lack of strength, not a lack of knowledge, but rather a lack in will."—Vince Lombardi

"The more you say, the less people remember."—Francois Nefelon

"Don't ask for a light load, but rather ask for a strong back." —Jewish Proverb

"Challenges are what make life interesting; overcoming them is what makes life meaningful."—Joshua Marine

"Take the first step in faith. You don't have to see the whole staircase, just take the first step."—Martin Luther King, Jr.

• • • • • • • •

Thursday August 30, 2007

Subject: So my white blood cells are mean....

....because they decided to kick out Nerdy and Rainbow. Apparently they decided they weren't good enough.

Anyways, that basically means that my white blood count has dropped. It's at 0.4, ouch! I still feel ok though. I'm getting the works today at MD. Three different chemos and an antibiotic. That's a lot of gross stuff. The doctors decided to hold my shots (*thank Jesus!*). My poor mom, she hates giving me the shots and I hate getting them. My stomach looks like I got attacked with a paintball machine because of the bruises.

Moving on, I thought I would share this with you.

I was talking to a friend of mine that I graduated high school with. She was diagnosed with Leukemia back in March and was in ICU for two months getting treatment. Anyways, the treatment she got didn't make her lose her hair, and she is doing better, but she hates getting the chemo. As I was talking to her, I realized how discouraged and negative she was about the whole thing, when things could be *so* much worse. Like losing your hair. I tried telling her that she shouldn't be so negative, and try to look on the bright side. There are so many different reasons to be discouraged when you are diagnosed with cancer. Like I have said before, many look at it as a death sentence. She was talking about how she was just so angry that it happened to us when we were 21, that these were the years that we were supposed to experience college and life, but instead we have this cancer deal over our heads for the rest of our lives. I realized that attitude really does make a difference. I've decided that even when I feel sick, I need to look on the bright side. This phase is almost done! And then it's just a few more months and I'm done. I told her that ya, it really sucks that it happened, but you can't be negative about it because all it's going to do is bring you down. So, that's Lauren's lesson for today. When you are down, don't worry, it will be ok.

Me and my mom are doing just fine in our home away from home. One of my best friends from high school lives here in Houston and is about five minutes away from us. She has a big DVD collection, so she has become our Blockbuster. So far we have watched the entire first season of Nip/Tuck because we have nothing better to do. We have kind of started to venture out a little bit and explore Houston, and by that I mean driving two blocks farther than we usually do. We found a Barnes and Noble, Wells Fargo and some other neat shops to entertain us.

We are hoping to go home on Wednesday of next week. Eric's birthday is on Thursday and my mom's is on Friday. Hopefully we will be able to go home!

Anyways, that is the latest!! Love choo all!!
Lauren

"It's not just in some of us; it's in everyone. And as we let our own light shine, we unconsciously give other people permission to do the same."–Marianne Williamson

"A good laugh and a long sleep are the best cures in the doctor's book."–Irish Proverb

"From the bitterness of disease man learns the sweetness of health."–Catalan Proverb

• • • • • • •

Wednesday September 5, 2007

Subject: What? Ya'll want an e-mail from me? Crazies.

Well, my white blood cells decided to not be loners anymore and invited along some more friends, Pepsi, Taco and Bell. My WBC is up to 1.0! WAHOO! Way better than 0.4. Ouch. While those are getting better, my platelets have fallen off the band wagon. They were down to 10,000 yesterday. Normal is anywhere from 150,000-400,000, at least I think.

So, what does that mean? Well, there is good news and bad news. Let's start off with the good news first shall we?

I get to go home today! Ahhhh, home. My sparkling city by the sea, I miss you! Me and my mom for sure thought that we had to stay until at least Thursday, but by the grace of God Dr. Thomas, who likes to keep me hostage here in Houston, agreed to let me go home and finish chemo in Corpus. I have been to the hospital every day since we got here to Houston, starting with the actual hospital stay and then going for at least an hour every day for antibiotics or chemo. In fact, I have to be there in about an hour.

More good news? I'm starting to feel *better*. I don't feel great, but I feel decent. Yesterday I had a platelet transfusion and since then I have felt ok.

Good/Bad News? My Lovenox shots are still on hold. I don't care what you people say, those shots *hurt*. I don't know if you know, but I weigh like 104 pounds and I never thought I would say this, but I wish my belly I had from when I was taking steroids would come back. My body has returned to normal and that means those shots hurt. Enough said. The bad news about that? The shots were good because they helped prevent blood clots. Hopefully now that I'm back on my feet I won't even have to worry about dumb blood clots.

Ok, the bad news? Remember a while back when I was hospitalized for that extreme body pain I had? Where you couldn't even like touch my arm without me being in excruciating pain? I'm going to have that again. We later learned that all that pain was due to my bone marrow kicking into overdrive and all my white blood cells coming back (something along those lines). Well, since I'm getting better, all that muscle pain is coming back. The good news? Now we have pain killers that aren't like water and actually do something.

I'm so excited to get this phase over with. It's been a long two months. Like I said, Thursday is officially the last day of my chemo for Consolidation 1. It's also my little "big" brother's birthday! He is going to be 16, unreal. My mom's birthday is the next day. She says to tell you she will be 32.

Yesterday, we had this great nurse who was just super funny and really easy to get along with. She started talking to my mom about the news, and my mom mentioned something about the insane amount of crime that happens in Houston. The nurse started talking about it, and then started talking about the crime that was happening in New Orleans. My mom asked her if she was in Houston because of Hurricane Katrina, and she said yes. She started telling us about how she lost her home and her belongings. When she did find another place to live she was just grateful to have a place to sleep and work. People like that amaze me because even though everything was taken away from her, she still managed to have a great sense of humor and was able to put other people at ease by being herself.

Anyways, my point is, and I think I may have mentioned this before, forgive me sometimes my brain doesn't work the way I want it to, things happen, and even though your entire world falls apart, everything else goes on without you. Here I am, *thrilled* to be going home, and all I can think about is meeting up with my friends, getting dressed normally (and by that, I mean wearing something other than pajamas), going to church or out to eat. But then you start to think about it and you come to the slow and painful realization that even though my life (as well as my family's) has been completely put on hold, everything and everyone around us moves on. New things happen that you don't know about, and you begin to get "out of the loop" about a lot of things. All you want is some type of normalcy, but the normalcy that you have come to know involves going to the hospital every day or sitting in a hotel room. It's pretty sad when the highlight of your day is being able to go to Target.

Once again (I never really get to the point I just keep rambling), even though everything is completely different, you have to choose what you are going to do. You can either shrivel up and let people think, "Oh ya, remember her/him? This happened, and things haven't quite been the same." Or you can say, ok, stick my head out there and *force* myself to show others, hey, I'm still me. So what I have a million different weird chemicals in my body, or new scars and no hair. I'm still me. So when I come home, don't act like I have brain damage (ok, maybe just a little), but pick things up where they left off. You don't have to skirt around the issue of where I have been or what I have been through since June, you just have to embrace it like I did.

Ok, I don't know if that really had a point, but sometimes I just think a lot and this is the result of it. I love choo all and I'll be home soon!
Lauren

"Life is going to shovel dirt on you, all kinds
of dirt. The trick to getting out of the well
is to shake it off and take a step up. Each of
our troubles is a stepping stone. We can get out
of the deepest wells just by not stopping,
never giving up! Shake it off and take a step up."- Unknown

• • • • • • •

Wednesday September 12, 2007

Subject: This is the song that never ends.

Seriously.

I'm beginning to think that I'm allergic to Corpus Christi or something. Which would be bad. I haven't really written much because ever since we have been home I have been pretty down and out. I either over did it or caught a bug or something. We came home about a week ago, and I had my last chemo on Thursday. So, that's good news! This cycle is done! *jumps around and does a happy dance*. Thursday I felt pretty darn good, and Friday I felt good enough to go to the football game (which was awesome, go brother!). I guess I got a little bit ahead of myself or something by thinking that because my counts were going up, I could kind of go back to normal. Big mistake.

I woke up Saturday morning feeling pretty nauseated, and since then I have had a rough time keeping food down. The poor Graham boys, not only have I been sick, but my mom has been pretty sick also. They sure have been having fun taking care of us two pathetic people. We are beginning to think that maybe we caught some kind of bug, because it seems like we have a lot of the same symptoms. She keeps joking and saying that she has "sympathy pain."

My platelets are super low again, so I'm bruising super easy. Bummer. I have a bunch of bruises on my chest from paper tape, ya, you heard right. Paper tape. Because my counts were so low, they also put me back on those neupogen shots (UGH). I used to be able to handle shots and needles pretty well, but I tell you what, I am such a big baby now. I can't stand shots or needles. I usually end up singing some type of song that goes along the lines of "I hate shots, ow ow ow I hate shots ow ow ow is it over yet?!" And then they put a pink Barbie band-aid on it.

So because I'm on the neupogen, my counts are going up (we think) which is causing all the bone pain. I have a lot of pain in my chest, kind of in the sternum area, well, pretty much everywhere there is a bone. So, imagine your skeleton, then imagine every single bone you have hurting. No bueno. My stomach feels like it's been hit by an 18-wheeler.

But anyways those are all the latest symptoms. I'm crossing my fingers and hoping that I get better soon because I want to hang out with people! I find myself becoming more and more irritated with those that are close to me, and I don't mean to do that. So if I have done that, I really am sorry. I constantly find myself trying to make sure that those around me are happy, because I want to be happy. So, if you are around me, no excuses, be happy! I like to laugh! But ya, I do feel bad about snapping at people. Bear with me. You know it's not like me to normally be that way!

I do believe that is all, my friends. I really do enjoy hearing back from ya'll. I know I don't write back sometimes, but I like to know how others are doing and what is new with everyone. I have blood work again tomorrow so keep your fingers crossed that my counts are up! Keep those prayers up that I can keep the right attitude about everything, that I can catch myself when I'm being grouchy, that my mom starts to feel better...ahh the list goes on and on. I love you all very much!

As my cousin Gillian says... "love ya oodles and noodles!!"
Lauren

I love this one...

"People are often unreasonable and self-centered. Forgive them anyway.
If you are kind, people may accuse you of ulterior motives. Be kind anyway.
If you are honest, people may cheat you. Be honest anyway.

If you find happiness, people may be jealous. Be happy anyway. The good you do today may be forgotten tomorrow. Do good anyway.

Give the world the best you have, and it may never be enough. Give your best anyway.

For you see, in the end, it is between you and God. It never was between you and them anyway."–Mother Teresa

• • • • • • • •

Tuesday September 18, 2007

Subject: Party on white blood cells!

Oh ya, my white blood cells have *finally* come out of hibernation. And man oh man, they are celebrating! Here is the rundown of the past week.

As most of you know, last week I was having a lot of problems eating and just not feeling good. My counts were really low even though I was having the neupogen shots. In fact, they were dropping. Not by much, but when you only have like, two white blood cells it makes a big difference!! Friday night my stomach was just in shambles, I could barely even stand up straight! I tried medicine, I tried soaking in a hot bath, nothing was working. Me and mom headed out to the E.R. Everyone was great, I didn't have to wait or anything and they gave me pain medicine right away.

Anyways, I was admitted. I've been getting neupogen shots every day along with pain/nausea medicine through my IV and fluids. I started to feel a little bit better, but my counts were still really low. I had a platelet transfusion and right now I am getting a blood transfusion. My bone pain has come back, and geeeeeeeez it hurts! But it's ok, my white count went from 1.4 to 4.4 in a day! So, I'm pretty sure that all those white blood cells are dancing and jumping around in there, which is making me hurt.

I've been in an isolation room the whole time so far, so anyone who has to come visit me has to wear a mask and gloves. That always cracks me up to see other people wearing them! Thanks to everyone who came to visit me, it's always nice to get a good laugh. And if you came to visit me the first day I was here, I do apologize for being *very* cranky. I came to the hospital for nausea, and they told me that I had to drink this awful drink for the catscan. It tasted like metal and crystal light. Disgusting.

81

So, I should be able to go home tomorrow. I want to make sure that I have this pain under control before we come home so I won't be miserable! I'm so excited because we don't have to go back until Monday or Tuesday, so we have a few days of hopefully feeling pretty good! That's all I have for now, my mind just went completely blank!

Love choo alll......
Lauren

"Let no one ever come to you without leaving better and happier."
–Mother Teresa

• • • • • • • •

Sunday September 23, 2007

Subject: Update

A lot has happened since the last email. Hope you have a few minutes to read this one!

Last time I talked to ya'll, my counts were doing better and I was hoping to get out of the hospital. Change of plans. On Wednesday? Or was it Thursday? Who knows. I signed my discharge papers and while I was waiting to go home, I ended up falling asleep and napping. When I woke up, I felt kind of hot and my mom wanted to take my temperature, and sure enough I had a fever. I never have a fever, ever! So, I ended up having to stay an extra couple of days to make sure it wasn't anything too bad. I finally got to go home on Friday, and it has been great being home.

Today was an awesome day because I finally got to go to church! I cannot begin to explain how great it is to walk in those doors and see that beautiful stained glass. There is just such a feeling of comfort and peace there. I miss it!

People have been asking how I have been feeling, so I will gladly tell you. I'm ok. I'm not a 100%, but I'm ok. I do get tired very easy, but one of my biggest problems is still the bone and muscle pain. Think about it, you go through your whole life walking, running, building up your muscles in your legs. I was constantly on the go before, ok, maybe I was kind of lazy, but still. Waiting tables requires lots of walking around! Anyways, my point is, laying around for the past three months has done nothing for my muscles. It is to the point where I can't bend down to get something without some serious support to get back up. We are going to look into physical therapy to work on that but we'll see. I still have some problems with nausea, but I don't expect that to go away. So, in a nutshell...I'm ok.

We leave for Houston tomorrow. *yay* (gag me).

I have no idea how long we will stay there. Tuesday is the big day. Lots of prayers, por favor. I have another PET scan to see if the cancer is in any of my lymph nodes, more blood work, and another bone marrow biopsy to see if that 2% is gone. Holy goodness gracious I am *not* looking forward to that biopsy. I have worked myself up over it (which I usually don't do but for some reason I have), and even though I can't see what they are doing, just the thought of having a huge needle pushed in your hip/bone/whatever....gross. I'll definitely send ya'll another email on Tuesday to let you know the game plan from then on out.

Like I said, we got to go to church today. Every song that we sang, every person that I saw, every word that was said, I am so thankful for. We sang songs about just being thankful and counting blessings. You never know what is going to happen in your life, and you never know when it is going to hit. Your entire world can be completely turned upside down in 2.5 seconds, and you think, ok, this is now my burden, this is my problem, but you have to look at the positive. You *have* to. It isn't just your problem, it becomes your family, your friends, your church, your enemies, and it becomes something that everyone thinks about. I'm not trying to be, what's the word here, selfish? But it's true. All the times you think, why me, why did I have to get taken away from the things I love to do. It's going to be ok. It's still there. Sometimes the physical aspects aren't, but the love and support is. The foundation that you had before, it's still there. At least in my case it is, and every day I am more and more thankful and appreciative of what I have.

So, talk to you all again in a couple days!
I love choooooooooo alll!!!!!!!! oodles and noodles!
Lauren

"Have accountability - it challenges you to better your walk with God."–Unknown

I know I have used this before, but I don't care. I still love it and say it every day.

"No one can measure the depths of His understanding, He gives power to those who realize they have NO power."–Isaiah 40:29

• • • • • • • •

Tuesday September 25, 2007

Subject: Yup....

Sooooooo..........

All the scans came back negative!!!! Which means no more cancer!

jump around, dance a bit, jump some more

And we get to go home again! Shortest trip ever. And we don't have to go back until October 9th!

But the bad news is I still have to go through all the treatments, and I have to be put back on the Lovenox shots twice a day.

Huge update will be later I assure you. I'm just happy right now!

Love choo allllllll
Lauren

• • • • • • •

Thursday September 27, 2007

Subject: What cancer can NOT do

A friend of my mom's gave me a necklace that has the saying... "what cancer cannot do..." and it gave me the idea for an email. Even though I sent out the great news about being cancer free, that doesn't mean that the road ahead isn't going to be hard. It's a huge bummer to know, ok I'm finally starting to feel better, but in a few weeks time I'll be getting more and more chemo to make sure it doesn't come back, which means many more sleepless nights and days of being in bed sick. I am so happy to know that the actual cancer has been beat, but I don't want to give people a false sense of belief that everything will automatically return to normal, because it won't. It will eventually, but until then, I still need all the support I can get. I love you guys, and I hope you enjoy the little tag-a-longs I wrote out with the rest of it...

WHAT CANCER CAN NOT DO (original by Bob Gotti)....–Lauren's version

...invade the soul...I still have the same soul that I did. I like to think that I am still care-free, and although my heart may be heavy with worry at times, there is nothing anyone can do to take away my humor. At least I think I'm funny. Let me keep on believing that!

...suppress memories.....Cancer messes with your body physically, and at times it can make your brain act weird, but that doesn't take away any of my memories. Nothing will take away the memories of singing Celine Dion at the top of my lungs with Jamie and Dom on the way to Houston, or acting like a Spartan cheerleader with my brother, or any of the other good times I have with my family and friends.

...kill friendship...no way Jose. In case you don't know, I have pretty much the coolest friends ever. Who could ask for anyone better? Really, noise complaints for singing the soundtrack of "Little Mermaid"? Who else does that? I have girlfriends that I can talk to at anytime, and I'm honored to be able to say that many of my family members (you know who you are! The list is endless) are some of my best friends. It makes me smile to see those green and orange bracelets they are wearing in my honor.

...destroy peace...at times, it can lower you down and get you depressed, but no matter what, everything is at peace with me. Despite all the things I go through, I'm still at peace, to a point. I still hate shots. Seriously, I think I need to be hypnotized or something.

...conquer the spirit.....My spirit will never be conquered because I love God more than anything. If I let cancer take over my spirit, do you really think I would be sitting here writing you this? No. I wouldn't. I would have given up by now. It certainly would have been easier to do so.

...shatter hope...you *have* to have hope. Without it, how are you going to get through each day? How are you going to get out of bed each day? Hope is everything. You hope for the best, you pray for the best and God takes care of you.

...cripple love...if not, it makes it stronger. If he can see me like this, at my absolute worst, and still love me and appreciate me and tell me every day, I'm positive that love isn't crippled. He still thinks I'm beautiful with no hair or makeup, when I haven't been able to take a shower in three days because I can't get out of bed, and when I'm being my goofy self throwing food at him in his kitchen to get a laugh. He could have easily walked away, and he chose to stay. No, cancer won't cripple love.

...corrode faith...once again, it makes faith stronger. Like I have said, you can sit and question it, and wonder, why me? But that won't do anyone any good. You should be thankful that God put this on your shoulders to help other people in the future. He doesn't give you more than you can handle, but that doesn't mean He is going to make it easy for you.

...steal eternal life...I know where I'm going when I die. (Not that that is anytime soon!) Do you?

...silence courage....Every person who goes through this battle shows their courage. It's not just me, it's my mom, dad, Eric, Sean, my entire family. They show courage by sticking by me no matter what, by giving me the extra push when I need it, and by giving me constant love and support.

I love choo alll........
Lauren

• • • • • • •

Tuesday October 9, 2007

Subject: I'm back....

In Houston!

We just had our appointment with the doctor. Everything is going great! Both the bone marrow biopsy and the PET scan showed no signs of cancer anywhere. Whew! My counts are somewhat better, but still pretty low. They are good enough to start chemo today though. Here is the breakdown of the next few weeks.

I have chemo today, October 18, October 30, November 8 and November 20, give or take a few days and depending on what my counts decide to do. The great news about this is that after this cycle, I only have two months left! *runs around and dances*

There are a few downfalls to this cycle though. The biggest one (and it's soooooo gross) is methotrexate. I've had this before (It's the chemo that they give me in my spine), but this time not only am I getting it as a lumbar puncture, but also as an IV drip into my central line. A big side effect of the IV drip is mouth sores, so I have to seriously rinse my mouth out with the gross tasting mouth wash like 9483569873 times a day.

Also, they are upping my dosage of Vincristine (the chemo that causes my fingers and toes to go numb). The doctors had decided to cut it in half a few months ago because the numbness in my fingers was awful, so they are going to try and see how I react to it now.

I only have to have two lumbar punctures, and I'm getting one of them today. Today will be the longest (I'm having 4 different chemo's....wahhhhhhhhhhhh)

On the other hand, this cycle won't be too rough because it's so spaced out. We only have to come up the day before and if things go well, we should be able to come home the day after. It was sooo great to not have any chemo for a month, because things kind of went back to normal. My hair is growing back (go me!) and my hand-writing doesn't look like a 1st-grader anymore. Keep the prayers up that I can tough it out just a few more months and that I don't get completely knocked down like I did before.

I really enjoyed my time home, and I can't wait to go back. My little brother has had some problems with a small hernia in his stomach (I know, I know, his stomach? You all know that us Graham kids are definitely not normal), so he has been in a lot of pain the past few weeks. He needs to get better because he cracks me up with his physical humor (you know, dancing around like an idiot).

Other than that, everything is fabulous.

Love choo allllllllllllllllllllllllllllllllllllllllllllll
Lauren

"Some people find it hard to be both comedic and serious, though life manages it easily enough."–Unknown

"A good friend is cheaper than therapy and much more fun!" –Author Unknown AMEN!!

• • • • • • • •

Friday October 12, 2007

Subject: Mid-week update, if ya want

So, I was feeling pretty down and blah today.

I definitely got spoiled this past month not having to worry about chemo. A lot of people were worried that I was doing too much, or not paying attention to my counts. I was, I promise! Hear me out.

Wednesday night, I went to church. (This is a big deal for me because I've only been able to go a few times in the past few months!). It was so much fun to be back in that environment and to be surrounded by those people. I find myself constantly talking about my cancer though, because I have figured out that a lot of people skirt around it, or look at you funny. So, what do I do? I deal with it the best way I know how. Me and my brother were in the car, and I was asking him if I had offended people, and he said he wasn't sure but that it definitely made people uncomfortable when I whip off that bandana and show off my "hair".

It got me thinking. Are people uncomfortable about it because they don't understand it? Any takers? That's something I don't understand very well myself, but I would rather people come up to me and ask me questions, instead of looking at me like I'm some type of foreign thing and then talking about me when I leave.

Anyways, back to church. I know I have harped on it before, but I seriously adore this church and the people in it. It was awesome to go and sing and hang out with old friends and what not. Like I said, I have been feeling pretty blah the last few days because of the chemo, and the worst part about that is knowing, hey, I don't have cancer anymore, but they are still going to pump me full of the crap that makes me feel awful. It makes me nauseous, it gives me headaches, and I feel useless because I lay in bed all day.

But, I feel slightly better. A lot of you know that I was going to go to camp with the youth group this past summer, but I wasn't able to because of good ole cancer. Anyways, at camp, everyday they have a new video of all the shenanigans that go on during the day, Eric had sent me the last video from camp (It's somewhere on YouTube), but I never really watched the whole thing because it kind of upset me that I couldn't be there. Well, today I was online, and I came across the video and watched it. And there, at the very end, was my youth group, saying they loved me, they missed me and they wished that I was there at Zephyr 2007. *tear*

So, my point is, that even when I'm feeling awful and left out because I can't be where I want to be, I still have people who care and love me, and that means so much to me.

Other than that, that's all I got going on. Mucho prayer requests that I will start to feel better. I'm really worried because the past few days I have had a headache and I'm just crossing my fingers that it isn't a spinal headache. Gross. And another big issue at the moment is school. I need/want to go back, but my chemo more than likely is going to run through January, and me and my parents can't afford to drop classes again (we have had to drop the last two semesters). So, pray to good ole Jesus that I can go back to school! I want to graduate!!

I love chooooooooooooooooo all!!
Lauren

• • • • • • • •

Sunday October 21, 2007

Subject: Enough is enough!

I'm sorry if this e-mail comes across as sarcastic or whiny, but ya'll know me, sometimes I just have to tell you how I feel!

Like I said, enough is enough! I have come to realize that the hardest part of having cancer is not even having it anymore. When the cancer was at its peak, back when I had 834487509 lymph nodes that were swollen and what not, that was a piece of cake. When they first said, "Ok Lauren, this is what you have and what we have to do..." of course it was not fun to hear, but you still put on your big girl attitude and tough it out. And now? I am so sick and tired of being sick and tired (yup, I stole that from a song!)

I try so hard to put on a smile and be happy, and 97% of the time, I am! But what about those times when I'm not happy? These past few weeks have been really really hard on me. I'm so ready for it to be done and over with, and I know I'm almost there, but it's one of those things You can finally see the light at the end of the tunnel but it's kind of overcast. (That made sense in my head, hopefully you can see what I'm saying!) I sit here and think about the future, and I know in my heart that this whole experience will help another person, but it is such a frustrating process. My whole family has had their entire life put on hold, and that's just not cool.

This round of chemo really isn't that bad, and I shouldn't be complaining, but I have had a really hard time with reflux and my chest hurting. And of course, being tired. Other than that, I'm pretty spiffy.

I don't even know what it is like to be normal anymore and I know that I will never be normal again. Ok, ok, I know some of you are thinking. She wasn't ever really normal.

But do you see what I mean? I don't remember what it feels like to go a day without pain or a day going to school and so and so on. Deep down, I know that for whatever reason, God is putting me through this test. Sometimes I wish I could just call Jesus up and be like, "Hey buddy....umm....want to help explain this one to me?" It's getting harder and harder to not be able to do things that I want to do, go the places I want to go, you get the picture.

Ok, I think I am done ranting. Of course, I have a million other things that I can say, but I like to send you my emails so that you guys know that I'm ok, not down and blah. Tomorrow I will probably think to myself, probably shouldn't have sent that email out, just should have kept it in the draft folder! I hope that you all realize though how much these emails help me. Writing these out, and then hearing feedback from you, it really is kind of cool. It's my own kind of medicine.

Love choooooooooo all!
Lauren

• • • • • • •

Wednesday October 24, 2007

Subject: Iodine anyone?

First of all, thank you to everyone who sent encouraging messages my way this past week! I really appreciate it!

Last night me and my mom ended up going to the emergency room around 4 am. She had flushed my catheter earlier that night, and ever since she had it had been bothering me so we decided better safe than sorry, get it checked out. When we walked in, of course our nurse was this awesome guy who had taken care of me before. Anyways, they did the usual, catscan, blood work...... well....

While they were doing the Catscan, they had to inject the iodine. Story of my life, as they are injecting it, one of the lumens on my catheter pops right off and iodine goes all over my neck, back and face. That would happen to me right? It doesn't hurt or anything, it's just really sticky. The other catheter eventually worked, they gave me some pain medicine, and I was good to go. So, it's a good thing we did go get it checked out because the catheter is loose and needs to be repaired or replaced. That's the latest in my day!

I love chooo all!
Lauren

"I could go through this day oblivious to the miracles all around me or I could tune in and 'enjoy'."–Gloria Gaither

• • • • • • • •

Thursday October 25, 2007

Subject: How do they do it?

So, it seems that lately we have had more bad days than good. Tonight, I was starting to get over the nausea, so I decided to take a bath, but it seems like all the hot water just made my bones come alive. I've been in severe pain now for a few hours, and so far the pain medicine isn't doing much. The best way that I can describe it is that your muscles and bones are like melting together. Ouch!! Anyways, I've done enough complaining in my last few emails, and that isn't what this one is about.

Me and my mom were laying in bed (lately we have had little "slumber parties", she'll sleep in my room in case I need anything) and she had brought in a pocket promise book and another book. She told me that we should read a few before we fell asleep to try and distract me from the pain. So we sat there, just going back and forth with quotes from this book she had or verses from my Bible. The whole time, it made me so happy to know that my family does have faith to lean on, and it led me to the question, how do these other people do it?

I know that not everyone has let themselves meet up with God, and I know that there are a ton of people who do not believe. How do they get through their day? I don't know what I would do if I didn't know that God had His promise for me. Some people could counter-argue that and say, well, if God loved you so much then why would He put you through this? It's to make my faith stronger, and to show those who don't believe that it is a good thing to put all of your faith and understanding into God. So, take a minute and thank Jesus that you know Him and love Him, and as you go through the day, I bet you will notice the little things that He does for you.

I just wanted to share that with you guys tonight. It made an impact on me, so I figured it might do the same for you. Also, I'll leave you with some of the verses that we were going back and forth with.

Love choo allllllll
Lauren

"I am not saying this because I am in need, for I have learned to be content whatever the circumstances. I know what it is to be in need, and I know what it is to have plenty. I have learned the secret of being content in any and every situation, whether well fed or hungry, whether living in plenty or in want. I can do everything through him who gives me strength." Philippians 4:11-13 (NIV)

"But I will restore you to health and heal your wounds, declares the Lord." Jeremiah 30:17 (NIV)

"But he was pierced for our transgressions, he was crushed for our iniquities; the punishment that brought us peace was upon him, and by his wounds we are healed." Isaiah 53:5 (NIV)

"A righteous man may have many troubles, but the Lord delivers him from them all; he protects all his bones, not one of them will be broken." Psalms 34:19-20 (NIV)

"I say to my God my Rock, why have you forgotten me? Why might I go about mourning, oppressed by the enemy? My bones suffer mortal agony as my foes taunt me, saying to me all day long, where is your God? Why are you downcast, O my soul? Why so disturbed within me? Put your hope in God, for I will yet praise him, my savior and my God." Psalms 42:9-11(NIV)

• • • • • • • •

Monday October 29, 2007

Subject: Late night prayer requests

Hello friends....

We are back in Houston tonight. I need your prayers, big time. I'm not feeling good, at all. My legs are hurting me so bad, despite all the pain medication I've been taking all day. We ended up having to go back to the emergency room on Saturday for the leg pain. So that's my biggest worry right now. My legs have gone stupid on me! That's all I've got for now. Chemo in the morning, same ole drill. I'll keep you in my thoughts if you keep me in yours!

Love choo allllllll
Lauren

• • • • • • • •

Saturday, November 3, 2007

Subject: New Update

I will start with this.

"And when you're in a Slump,
You are not in for much fun. Un-slumping yourself
is not easily done."- Dr. Seuss

This past week has been rough. Seems like I have been starting off a lot of my emails that way lately huh? I don't mean to be depressing, but I do get depressed at times. I want this all to be over with, and I sat here and thought, I can write another discouraging email, or I can write about what I feel. Here's what I feel.

I still get very confused at God. That doesn't mean that I love Him any less, but I still question His actions. Why is this happening to me? I know some of you are thinking, jeez girl, cheer up. I'm cancer free, I'm in a lot better shape than most people are, but I still can barely get out of bed and what not. If you don't know by now, I have had four ER visits in about a week, all for the same thing. Good ole chest pain.

I've seen three different doctors, and had three different diagnoses, ranging from anxiety, chest wall pain and bone pain. I'm just a painful kind of girl. The fourth doctor decided that instead of just drugging me up and sending me home, to go ahead and admit me to get to the bottom of this dumb problem. So at the moment, I'm in a lovely hospital bed. Yup, the loud girl you hear down the hall, that's me. Like I said, once you are in a slump, it just gets harder and harder to get out of it. I have crawled out of my little slump though.

Last night was awful, but I definitely have a funny story that will make most of you laugh. They gave me a lot of medicine to try and control my pain, along with IV fluids, so my drugged up self kept having to get up and go to the bathroom. Anyways, outside my room there was a cop who was talking to my dad, and the cop was the guy who bought our old house. Well, I walked up to him, shook his hand, and then told him, "Sorry, I'm a bit high at the moment". Then I turn to my mom and said, "I just told a police officer that I was high." HA!

Love choooooo all!!
Lauren

• • • • • • •

Monday November 5, 2007

Subject: Quick update

Ok here's the latest that I know.

They did an ultrasound of my gallbladder, which came back completely normal. Tomorrow I have to have an Upper Gastrointestinal Endoscopy, which just sounds gross. They stick a metal tube that has a light and tiny video camera on the end of it (called an endoscope) down my esophagus and check out that, my stomach and the first part of my small intestine just to make sure that there aren't any ulcers, tumors, infections, you get the picture.

And I'm awake during it. Heavily sedated, but I'm freaking out about the thought of something being stuck down my throat. Oh good lord Jesus I'm freaking out about it! I'm sure it's just nothing, and it's a really super common procedure, but it's not something I want to have! If everything looks ok after my endoscopy tomorrow, I might get to go home, so I'm really excited about that!

Anyways, please pray for me. I can't eat anything past midnight except a breakfast of liquids, and I'm already craving a potato, egg and bacon breakfast taco. Trust me, I was eating until midnight. I was so full of food at midnight I thought I would never be hungry again! Oh lordy tomorrow is going to not be a fun day. I think that I'm scheduled for the procedure around 3 in the afternoon so say a quick prayer for me around that time!

Love chooooo all!!
Lauren

"Lots of people want to ride with you in the limo, but what you want is someone who will take the bus with you when the limo breaks down."–Oprah Winfrey

"Praise Him for all that is in the past, and trust Him for all things to come.:"–Joseph Hart-"How Good is the God We Adore"

"Years teach us more than books."–Berthold Auerbach

"A loving heart is the truest wisdom."–Charles Dickens

• • • • • • • •

Wednesday November 7, 2007

Subject: Very long update, but an update!

Except when you *don't.* because, sometimes, you *won't.*
I'm sorry to say so but, sadly, it's true
that Bang-ups and Hang-ups
can happen to you."
–Dr. Seuss

So me and my homie Dr. Seuss have become pretty close lately.
I'm going to start with that quote because I want you all to
realize that sadly, it is true, bad things are going and will happen
to you. But here's what you do. You take the bad thing that has
happened, no matter what it is and A.) Give it to God (if you don't
believe in God come talk to me. Soon.) and B.) Realize that it will
soon pass.

This past week has pretty much been hell (excuse my french). I
have had so many tests run, a lot of blood taken, talked to way
too many doctors, signed too many papers, and gosh darn it, I'm
tired! Some of you know, some of you don't, but I was admitted
to hospital on Friday night after my *fourth* ER visit with no result.
First I was diagnosed with chest wall pain, bone pain, and then
muscle pain. Needless to say I have been somewhat miserable.
Good thing the nurses up on fourth floor treat me like a queen.
Anywho, let me begin to tell you about all the funtastic (*gag me*)
tests I got to take.

Ok, so I really only had like 3 tests. I had the endoscopy, which
turned up completely normal (I think I mentioned that in my last
email, forgive me, my brain seriously is just so tired right now
and I'm running into walls and stuff, you'd be laughing). They
had me have an ultrasound of my gallbladder (which by the
way I have named Galapagos the GB, don't ask, I tend to name

things. Remember Whitey, Nerdy, Flip and Flop the white blood cells?). The official results of that showed that I had very tiny sludge particles that could possibly be very early gallstones, but no gallstones showed up. Sludge is exactly what it sounds like, and that's the official medical term. Sludge. That's just a funny word.

Next we had the Hepatobiliary Scan, which is a test to see how well and if my buddy Galapagos functions properly. We'll get to that in a minute. Let me tell you about the just absolute best test of them all.

It's called a modified barium swallow, but what they should really call it is let's see how long the patient can down this thick, disgusting, Mylanta textured drink. Seriously, imagine Mylanta that has been expired for 47 years and is super thick, and they expect you to drink this. I'm proud of myself for not throwing it up on the doctor, because that is exactly what I felt like doing. Anyways, after you drink the aged Mylanta, you have to drink the thinner version of it while you lay on a metal table

****(I'm sorry, I have extreme ADD and I'm listening to my iPod and "Old Time Rock and Roll" just came on, so excuse me, I'm dancing around and taking a break for a minute.)****

Ok, so you are lying on this extremely hard metal table (that is also below freezing since the radiology floor is like a permanent 20 degrees), and I had to lay on my right side while drinking the thinner barium from a straw. Then the doctor has me turn in two complete circles ("Turn on your back, now slightly onto your right side, now a little more, now on your stomach...." you get it.) The doctor made me do this because they were trying to determine if I had reflux or not, which I didn't. So, that test came back normal. By the way, Memaw hung out with me during most of these tests, so kudos to her!

Ok. Back to Test #2. They inject your chest with some dye that is supposed to light up your liver, your gallbladder, and your small bowel. Well, you see, my friend Galapagos is a little shy, because it never showed up, which means, you guessed it, my gallbladder doesn't function properly! My liver showed up immediately, and the small bowel showed up shortly after, and two hours later after the dye had already left my liver, little G still hadn't shown up. From what I understand, your small bowel is connected to your gallbladder by this thing called a cystic duct. Why does my GB not show up? Because there is some type of obstruction/blockage in that cystic duct. So, how do we fix it? Me and little Galapagos have to part ways. I was talking to my aunt earlier, and I told her all I wanted for Christmas was to have my gallbladder taken out! Seriously! So I'll keep you posted on when Galapagos has its funeral.

Here's the issue. Do we wait for chemo to be completely done with or can we possibly get it taken out after this phase of chemo is over? Not sure yet. We were supposed to go up to H-town today, but seeing that I just got discharged from the hospital, Dr. Thomas was super cool enough to let us catch our breath and come up next Tuesday, the 13th. Which means that my next chemo session should be scheduled for the 22nd, but since that's Turkey day, it will probably get pushed back to the 24th! Oh ya, two week break for me. Thank Jesus. After I got discharged today, my dad took me shopping (he hates shopping) and it was so awesome to have some quality father-daughter time. I definitely appreciate my parents more and more every day and try to tell them just how much I love them, but I don't think they will ever possibly realize it.

I know that this email has been super duper long, but I just wanted to update ya'll on everything that has been going on. I'm going to end with this. I have a prayer request for ya'll. One of my nurses is battling breast cancer for the second go round, has dealt with a brain tumor, and just started chemo again for cancer in her hip (I think it's her hip, I'm not exactly sure.) Anyways, she has been my nurse many times that I have been hospitalized, and she is just awesome. She makes me laugh, and she has given me a bunch of tips about dealing with cancer. Anyways, she is so inspirational because she works three days a week, and has four days off to rest from her chemo. She is *still working*. Pray for her that her journey, although it's going to be rough, that she can still keep up the great attitude and inspire others.

To those of you still reading, I love choooooo all!
Lauren

Yup, I still got quotes. I'm not skipping out on these!

"You are either part of the problem or part of the solution."
–Charles Rosner

"Life is what happens when you are busy planning it."–John Lennon

"Courage is being scared to death, but saddling up anyway."
–John Wayne

A long one, but a goodie. Last one, I promise

"The longer I live, the more I realize the impact of attitude on life. Attitude, to me, is more important than facts. It's more important than the past, education, money, circumstances, failures, successes, than what other people think or do or say. It's more important than being gifted or being skilled. It will make or break a company, a church, a home. The remarkable thing is we have a choice every day regarding the attitude we will embrace for that day. We can't change our past...we can't change the fact that people will act a certain way. We can't change the inevitable. The only thing we can do is play on the one string we have, and that's our attitude. I'm convinced that life is 10% what happens to me and 90% how I react. And with you-we are in charge of our attitudes."–Charles Swindoll

Ok I'm sorry for those who have spent the last 2 hours reading this ridiculously long email. I love you guys! Have a good day!

• • • • • • • •

Wednesday November 14, 2007

Subject: Peace out Galapagos!

Ugh, what a week!

We were back in the ER on Sunday morning with chest pain. It took four doses of pain medication to get it under control. The doctor that was on duty was the one that had figured out that it was my gallbladder a week ago, and she wanted to admit me then, but me and mom just decided to go home. (We were sleepy!)

Anyway, I ended up sleeping until like 8pm, and when I woke up, I ate a super low fat diet. Anything that is high in fat (they told me like more than 5 grams of fat) will make me sick. So, I was taking my medicine around the clock and doing what I was supposed to. I woke up Monday morning with chills and shakes, and sure enough I had a fever. We took more morphine and ativan, but nothing was working. Soon after that I ended up getting sick, and the chills and what not were pretty uncontrollable, so mom made the call to take me back to the ER. They admitted me when we got there, we finally got a room around 10:30, and the doctor on call told us that I definitely had to have gallbladder out. We were supposed to go to Houston yesterday though for chemo, but Dr. Thomas just told us to reschedule when I had kind of recovered a bit.

Everything went fine with the surgery (It was yesterday at 12:30). They weren't sure if they were going to be able to do it laparoscopically because my gallbladder was now infected. They were able to do it though! I have three little incisions on the right side of my stomach and one a little bit bigger right about my belly button. All they do is stick a tube with a camera on it in there and snip it out.

I didn't expect it to hurt this bad! Man oh man, it's rough. I feel like my stomach has been backed over with an 18-wheeler truck. Ouch! My mom and dad are hanging out with me all day today, which is good because I can barely get around.

That's the latest! I got my Christmas wish, to have Galapagos out! BRING ON THE THANKSGIVING FOOD!!!!

Love choooooooooo alllllllllllll
Lauren

"And in the end, it's not the years in your life that count. It's the life in your years."–Abraham Lincoln

"Though no one can go back and make a brand new start, anyone can start from now and make a brand new ending."–Carl Bard

• • • • • • • •

Monday November 19, 2007

Subject: Hola mis amigos!

Needless to say, it's been an interesting week.

I re-read the last e-mail that I sent out, and I realized that a lot of words were missing and I lost all ability to spell. Apparently being heavily medicated does that! Sorry!

Anyways, I'm doing better than I was. Finally no more chest pain! It's been a week since my gallbladder-ectomy (R.I.P Galapagos!) and I'm still a little sore, but I'm getting around a lot better. I have a little trouble taking in deep breaths and eating, but it is a zillion times better than it was, so I'm trying not to complain. It's nice to be at home and say ahh, no worries of going to the emergency room tonight!

Not too sure when we will start up chemo again. I have an appointment on November 29. I'm just so ready for it to be over. Only one more treatment after that, and then this phase is over. After that, it's only two more phases and then I hit maintenance. Super excited about that! Looking at the end of February or so to be done with it all, man oh man I can't wait!

Anywho, with it being Thanksgiving and all, I figured I would throw in my two cents. Or is it sense? I don't know. At church on Sunday, our pastor gave a message about "Thanksgiving Turkeys and Other Ungrateful People." He always has a slideshow with his message, and one of the questions that popped up was "What has God given you in the year 2007?" The first thing that came to my mind was, "Gee....God gave me cancer." Um, Ms. Negative much? Anyways, it's true. I mean, you all know how much I love God and would drop anything for Him, and I've never been angry at Him for this, but think about it. God ultimately is the one who decides who does what, when they do it, and why. So, I kind of got upset. I was sitting there thinking, God gave me cancer. It wasn't caused by me doing something wrong, or any of the other cancer myths that are out there. He said, okie, Lauren Graham..... she's going to get the big C. The pastor went on to talk about how Jesus provides a specific answer to a specific need and asking ourselves if we are truly thankful.

So, I went about my day still thinking about all of this and just kind of being mad at myself for even considering the thought of being mad at God. Why would I want to be thankful for getting cancer? But it hit me, I've said it before. Having cancer is like being in a club, whether you want to be in the club or not, you are a member. You can either choose to be negative about it, or you can step up and say, ok, if I have to be in this club I might as well be active in it. I don't have any other option. I have to be positive because I can't do this if I'm upset or sad. I just can't. Anyways, I don't know if that makes any sense, but it does to me, in the mind of Lauren!

I hope everyone has a fabulous Thanksgiving and eats a lot of food and football and shopping ads!

I love choo all!!!!!
Lauren

"We can make our plans, but the Lord determines our steps. Commit your work to the Lord, and then your plans will succeed. The Lord has made everything for his own purposes." Proverbs 16:9, 3-4 (NLT)

"Those who have a 'why' to live, can bear with almost any 'how.'" –Dr. Viktor Frankl

"Eyes that look are common. Eyes that see are rare."–J. Oswald Sanders

• • • • • • •

Monday November 26, 2007

Subject: Mini-update or something like that.

Heyyyyyyy everybody!

I was going to wait until Thursday to send out an update, but apparently you people like my e-mails so I'm back by popular demand.

Thanksgiving was great, and I hope everyone else had a good Turkey day also! As my mini-me cousin/"sister" said, "Happy Turkey Day! Gobble Gobble!" We had a really awesome time this weekend. It's been so nice to not be in the hospital, ER, cancer center, worrying about Galapagos, you get it! I finally had some down time to actually sit back and try to recover. We were able to go to the movies. Enchanted is super cute, everyone should see it. And the cashier lady asked how old I was. Had I been thinking I would have said 12 but in my defense I told her how old I actually was! We even braved a few stores, made it to church this morning. Overall a pretty good weekend.

I'll be honest though, I am not looking forward to Thursday. As time goes on and we get closer and closer to the end of this whole process, I find myself drawing back a little bit more each time we get ready to go to Houston. It's almost as if I'm at the end of my rope, and I have no idea how much I can give. The past month of issues that weren't necessarily related to MD Anderson have completely wore me down, and I worry that I won't be able to put on the brave face that I usually try to do. I don't know how people go through their battles for years with cancer. I've only been in it since May, and it's enough. I've been thinking a lot lately of how people react to cancer. I mean, be honest (I am!), how many of you out there think the most over-used statement - "Oh, that will never happen to me....cancer just happens to older people, or people who deserve it." Seriously! You know at some point or another, you have all thought that. Cancer is *everywhere* whether you want to see it or not. That doesn't mean it's a bad thing though. Even at the movies this weekend, one of the previews was about St. Judes and helping kids who have it. I don't really know what my point is, but I guess it is somewhere along the lines of don't take things for granted. I have been so grateful this past couple of weeks to somewhat live in normalcy, even if my normalcy now means being able to go more than one place a day, or getting excited over new scars (Four of them! All in one day!), or even just being able to go outside and notice what the weather is like. Who knows what I'm talking about now, at this point it's three in the morning, I can't sleep and I tend to write emails when I can't sleep because my brain is in overdrive.

Another cool highlight of this past week? A few days ago, my mom helped me cut off those last little hairs that were holding on for dear life. I no longer look like a rugrat who has stuck my finger into an electrical outlet! Go me!! Cross our fingers that my hair won't fall out again!

So, the plan is to drive to Houston on Wednesday, slammed with chemo on Thursday, and come home on Friday. I will try my best to send out another update Thursday after chemo. We know for sure that I am getting three different chemos through my IV and a lumbar puncture. So thrilled! *ya right.* The good news is that after this, only one more session of chemo and then I'm done with this phase. Anyways, enough out of me. I really should try and sleep!

Love chooo alll!!
Lauren

• • • • • • •

Saturday December 1, 2007

Subject: MD Anderson *gag me*

So we just came back from another lovely trip to Houston. It was an interesting one.

We were still unsure about what the doctors would decide about my chemo. Here is how it went down.

As most of you know, I'm in a pediatric protocol, so the research nurse for that study (Brenda) and my "adult" doctor (Dr. Thomas) communicate a lot. Usually in the protocol, if something happens to where the kids have to miss the chemo, they usually just skip it and go on to the next phase. Since I had surgery, Brenda was saying that normally, I would just skip this and go on to Consolidation 3A. Dr. Thomas thought it would be best if I went ahead and at least did one more round of this cycle, because she thought that the next phase would be too rough to do all at once. Dr. Thomas talked to the pediatric doctor, and she won. So, yesterday I went ahead and had a lumbar puncture and three different chemos.

Confused? Me too.

So, while we were in the office talking to Brenda, she was telling me how I wouldn't have to have any more bone marrow aspirations (they told me this a long time ago too!). Anyways, Yolanda (She's the lady who always calls me to tell me what time my appointments are. I finally met her yesterday for the first time, she's funny!) calls me today to tell me my schedule for next week. We weren't supposed to go back for ten days! Apparently, Dr. Thomas thinks that it would be wise to go ahead and restage the cancer, just to make sure that it really was my gallbladder this whole time. So guess what I get to do next Wednesday? A FRIGGIN' BONE MARROW ASPIRATION. I despise those. I think we

115

are going to try and get in touch with MDA to see if being sedated is possible. I'm such a wuss, but I can't take another BMA! They hurt! BAD!! So, I get another BMA, another PET scan, more lab work, and an echocardiogram just to make sure my heart works. And on top of that, I'm having some type of allergic reaction (I think) to the adhesive that holds my central line in place. Good news? My hair is growing back super fast. Go me. Bad news? Everyone has told me that the next phase will definitely cause hair loss. Maybe if I just concentrate *really* hard, I can convince all those hair loss medicines or whatever to just work on my legs and not my head!

Other that all of that, everything is going pretty well. I'm feeling pretty good so far, other than my back being sore. I don't know the schedule of my next phase yet, but once I know I'll let ya'll know. I won't get a break for Christmas though. Bummer. While we were there in Houston, we videotaped my lumbar puncture in different segments and took a bunch of pictures. Pretty neat to have that on record!

Love chooooooo all!!
Lauren

• • • • • • • •

Monday December 10, 2007

Subject: Say what?!

Hey friends!

It has definitely been an interesting week (seems my emails keep starting out that way, huh?). Quick health update, here we go. This last round of chemo has done me in. Chemo has always been rough, but I guess you begin to somewhat build up a tolerance for it. I hadn't had any for almost a month, so getting four doses of it definitely made me sick. We had a lot of problems with nausea and getting sick. Pretty much every side effect that they warn you about, I've had this week. Sunday night I was hospitalized again for abdominal pain. They let me go on Thursday. My white count is dropping again, along with all my other counts. *yay* Other than that, I'm feeling ok. Of course, seeing that it is two in the morning, I have quite a bit on my mind and I just thought I would share with you wonderful people.

I was able to go to church this morning. The church is decorated for Christmas (it's so pretty!), green wreaths, red banners, Christmas trees, beautiful stuff. Anyways, during church we sang the song that goes "Jesus, Jesus, Jesus...there's just something about that name....." It's been stuck in my head all day because my cousin Jennifer kept singing it after church, but instead of Jesus, she would insert someone else's name, and we were all laughing about it. As I sat there laughing, it dawned on me. It was the first time in a long time that I felt normal. I wasn't thinking about being sick, or about any of the other complications, I was just surrounded by my family and friends laughing and talking in this big beautiful church. I tell you what, this church inspires me so much. So many things have happened in that church. I can remember being a little girl, not wanting to go, so my mom would let me take coloring books, and then I would sleep throughout the whole service, and then I remember getting a little bit older

117

and starting to pay attention to the sermons, attending countless church plays, being in church plays, going to Sunday School, going to camps, getting baptized, getting recognized for graduation....I could go on and on about this place. I look forward to going to church because as I walk through those doors, there is a sense of relief. It's as if all my troubles are left at the door, and I can just be me there. It's a great feeling.

I tell you that because I know that I am fixing to go through a really hard time and I will need that normalcy and support more than ever. I keep telling everyone, I see the light at the end of the tunnel, but it's cloudy. I only have a few months left of chemo, but I have a feeling that it is not going to be easy at all. These past six months have flown by, and although I hope the next three will be just as quick, I feel like they are going to drag on forever. One of the hardest things is finally getting to a point where you are back in some type of routine, and then knowing that your routine is fixing to be completely turned upside down. I know we are fixing to enter back into that world where I sleep all day, if I'm able to eat a cup of soup it's a good day, and being separated from my family again. There are so many things that you never think about losing until you have lost them. I have realized that once you have cancer, at least with me, you lose a huge portion of your dignity.

But what can I do?

Stay positive. Keep laughing. Know that by wearing a Santa hat to chemo treatment will make someone there who is in the same boat as you smile. Know that somehow, someway, you can still help other people, even though you may not be there physically.

So, those are my thoughts for the night. It makes sense in my mind, and I know that I am just rambling on, but know that it makes me feel better to write it all out.

PET scan, blood work, bone marrow aspiration (hopefully with lots of sedation) on Wednesday. Results on Thursday. Will be sure to let you know!

Love chooooooo alllll!
Lauren

"God has blessed you so that you may bless others. Start sharing today!"–Unknown

"Faith is seeing light with the eyes of your heart, when the eyes of your body see only darkness."–Barbara Johnson

P.S. One of the first people who called me when I got diagnosed was a boy a few years younger than me who had already been through cancer. He had been diagnosed a few years before that, and he told me all about MD Anderson, what to look for, who to talk to, and was just super nice to me. Anyways, his cancer has come back in his lungs. Pray for this kid. I don't know him that well, but I know that he has big plans and doesn't deserve this.

● ● ● ● ● ● ● ●

Thursday December 13, 2007

Subject: Whoever thought a fake ribcage could be so cool?

Hey ya'll!

So here we are at lovely MD Anderson (I just love this place.)

Yesterday, we had all of my testing/restaging done. I had blood work, the echocardiogram and the dreaded bone marrow aspiration. This time, they gave me sedation. I was really worried about it because it was the same sedation that they used when I had my central line put in the first time (which did nothing). This time though, they actually waited like thirty minutes after they gave it, and they gave me two doses, so in my little sedated mind the aspiration seemed to go by a lot quicker. It still hurts like crazy though. In between the aspiration and the echocardiogram me and my mom went to this really cool museum here in Houston. We ventured out! The museum was set up like the inside of a human body. So cool. You got to walk around through these giant replicas like the mouth, the ribcage, the brain and all the major organs. My favorite part of the whole thing was in the ribcage room. They had a scanner that showed the entire body, and it showed what an x-ray, MRI, catscan, and PET scan looked like. Very interesting to see it all there and think, yup, I've had *all* this done before! I learned all about the gallbladder that I don't have any more, and they had life-size bodies all over the place that showed the insides of bodies, and one traced all the lymph nodes in a person's body. I could literally pick out all of my swollen ones! Only I could be excited about something like that.

Anyways, back to the good ole medical/restaging stuff. Everything looks great. My counts are way up since when I left the hospital, my echocardiogram looks perfect. I still have 1% of those blast cells in my bone marrow, but Dr. Thomas said that was completely normal. And I only have 13 more treatments and then I hit maintenance! GO ME! Can you say party? Here is how this round of chemo will go. (those still following, this is Consolidation 3A). Today, I have another lumbar puncture, Pegulated Asparaginase (or asparagus as we like to call it), daunorubicin, and vincristine. They say that the daunorubicin will for sure make my hair fall out again. Got to look at the bright side, at least I won't have to shave my legs for the next month again! They are also cutting my dose of vincristine in half because of all the dumb problems I had last week. Then, on the 20th and 27th, I have to come back to Houston to get checked out with Dr. Thomas and then I will get the vincristine and daunorubicin. I also have to take steroids again, but it's not near as bad as last time. It's only seven days on, seven days off, and then seven days on again. So, compared to some of the other brutal sessions, this really isn't *that* bad. Could be worse.

So, that's the latest from the continuing saga of Lauren. I'm super excited for Christmas (got all my shopping done, even if it means I only have $37 left in my bank account!), and I keep telling my mom that is going by all too quickly. We both vote that Christmas should last from the end of November to mid-March. I'll be sure to update ya'll again soon if anything interesting/unusual happens, and knowing me, I'm sure it will be soon. Merry Christmas!

Love choo alll..........
Lauren

This is my favorite song of the week. Explains everything perfectly. If you haven't heard it, go listen to it because I said so.

"Bring the Rain" Performed by MercyMe
Songwriters: Billy Montana/Helen Darling

I am Yours regardless of the dark clouds that may loom above
Because You are much greater than my pain
You who made a way for me by suffering Your destiny
So tell me what's a little rain

• • • • • • • •

Sunday December 16, 2007

Subject: Pirates, Mary and Joseph?!

Hey all.

I can assure you that the chemo is kicking in. Been feeling pretty puny the last few days, especially this morning. The choir at church today did their Christmas program and it was great to hear it.

Anyways, I'm dropping this quick email because I want to tell you something that happened at church. There is a little boy there at church, about three, and he thought that I was a pirate because I was wearing a red bandana. So what else is there to do but say "arggg" and say I'm sorry for not wearing my eye patch? He then wanted to spin me around in circles and look at my sparkly shoes. It's times like these when I like to see little kids. A lot of the time, they realize that there may be something different about you, but sometimes they can't really figure it out, so they just treat you like any other person, or a pirate. Gillian (my four year old cousin) refers to me as the "sister with funny hair", and to watch out, because her "sister is sick". Every time I talk to her she asks me if I feel better. Who would have thought being classified as a pirate at church would make me feel slightly better? Anyway, I thought that was a good story.

We go back to Houston on Wednesday for some more chemo. Hopefully everything will go ok. I'll be sure to let you know! Take time this Christmas season to remember what is important. Your family, your friends, and most importantly, the Savior that was sent to us on Christmas day. If that doesn't make you happy, I don't know what will!

Love choo all!!!!!!!
Lauren

• • • • • • • •

December 27, 2007

Subject: The never ending Saga from Houston!

What up home skillets?

I hope everyone had a great Christmas! I know I did. I got to hang out with my family. That tops it all. Gillian and I made a gingerbread house (the decorating was pretty pathetic because she just wanted to eat the candy and Denise had to deal with the messy frosting), we got to eat our little hearts out. Overall it was just really nice to be in everyone's company. The other piece of exciting news that we got today is that my brother, Eric, just passed his driving test, which means he is going to want to drive *everywhere* so watch out. I'm warning you now!

Here in Houston, me and mom are just sitting around waiting for chemo. It's been a long day. No one ever called us with a schedule, so we just assumed it was the same 8:00 am appointment that it always is. Of course, my appointment was at 7:00am, but we rolled in at 8:15. Didn't get blood work until 9, then we had to get a chest x-ray, wait an hour in Infusion Therapy so they could place an IV (they won't inject Iodine through my catheter anymore), then off to wait for another hour to get another CT Scan. Once again, I do not wish that on anyone. Having Iodine injected into your veins is one of the weirdest feelings ever. It burns, and it makes your whole body kind of warm up with it. No bueno. Anyways, everything came back great. We had the CT Scan in the first place to double check and make sure that the blood clot in my lung was gone (which it was). My counts have dropped a little bit, but not that bad. Best of all, I have a two week break! We don't have to come back to Houston until January 10, but when we do come back it's going to be kind of rough. Four days of treatment, three days of rest, and then four more days.

Only one downside this visit. Dr. Thomas has officially labeled me a "weird" patient. She can't explain the bone and muscle pain that I get after treatment sometimes, and there are lots of things that are kind of abnormal that she can't figure out. At least she is funny about it. She thinks that it's possible I had some type of chronic pain problem before I was even diagnosed (remember all those years of joint and muscle pain?) and the treatment just aggravates it. Next time we come up here she is going to try and set us up with a pain specialist to see if there is a way to get to the bottom of that problem.

It's hard to believe that I'm almost done. Today is the last treatment of Consolidation 3A. Only one cycle left! I've been going through all the old emails, and I can't believe that all of this stuff happened three, four, even six months ago! Crazy. I can't thank ya'll enough for sticking it out to see what happens. I'll be sure to update you guys again soon (knowing me, something is bound to happen that will be good enough reason for an email!)

Love choo all!!!!!!!!!!!
Lauren

• • • • • • • •

January 8, 2008

Subject: On the road again......

Hey everybody!

I'm back! We are heading back to Houston tomorrow for the last cycle of chemo. Can you believe it? Crazy to think that it has been eight months since this all started. I'm expecting this cycle to be kind of rough, so I've definitely been preparing for it. I lost about ten pounds last time, so I have been eating like crazy trying to gain some weight so that I don't wither away. I don't know that many details about it other than I have four days of chemo, three days of rest, and four more days. Me and my mom plan on staying up there in Houston for at least those eleven days. It will be the longest stay since our very first once back in June. Once I meet with the doctor on Thursday, I'll send out another email updating you guys on what is going on.

I did pretty good during the break. We only had one emergency room visit! I've had this problem with really severe back pain (like in the tailbone area), and last week it got to the point where it was pretty unbearable, so mom and dad decided it would be best to call an ambulance. I had to get two shots (they wouldn't give me pain medicine through my catheter because we had been taking it all day to try and control the back pain), one of Toradol and one of Valium. It took a few days for the pain to completely ease up, but I'm doing better now.

Everyone in the family is doing well. Eric is going to Pigeon Forge, TN on a mission trip next weekend, so pray that that trip goes well! Also, pray for my dad. He will be here by himself for five days, hopefully he won't get too bored! I'll send out another update soon!

Love choo alll..........
Lauren

• • • • • • •

January 10, 2008

Subject: And we were so close!

So, we packed our entire house, unpacked in the hotel room, spent $80 on groceries at Target for our twelve day stay here in Houston, and we are going home tomorrow.

Ahhh....we were so close!

Here is the rundown of what happened today/last night.

We saw a pain specialist today and learned a lot. Learned why certain medicines didn't work, learned what medicines we can take together without me getting too weirded out, learned why Motrin works better for my joint pain than the heavy duty narcotics. By the way, I can take Motrin again when I hit the maintenance phase which is awesome, because it's one of the few medicines that actually takes away my joint pain. Motrin has been a taboo drug during my chemotherapy. They suggested that I see a rheumatoid arthritis doctor when we get back to Corpus. Of course, let's just add that to the mix!

Here's the bad news. My counts aren't high enough to start chemo. So we can't start until the 22nd. I just have to have some more blood work done next week to make sure my counts are recovering.

About three days ago, we noticed that my catheter was kind of red and sore, so we decided to go ahead and watch it and make sure it didn't get infected. Well, last night we changed the dressing again, and it looked a lot more red and kind of inflamed. We told Dr. Thomas about it, and she suggested we go to Infusion Therapy. Just for the record, Infusion Therapy is now considered a bad word. If you say it, you get your mouth washed out with soap! It's the worst part of the whole hospital. You go sit and wait for hours just to be seen, ugh. Once we finally got in there, the nurses agreed that it would probably be best if it got taken out.

I'M SO EXCITED!!!!!!!!!!!!!!!!!!!!!!!!!

You don't understand, I've had this catheter in my chest since July 11, 2007. I can't take showers (only baths, and even then I'm supposed to put saran wrap over it), and it's gotten to be pretty painful in the last few days. So, we are coming home tomorrow and going straight to the hospital to get the catheter taken out. We can't get it taken out here in Houston because they placed it in Corpus and then they wouldn't send the orders because they said that MD Anderson wasn't associated with the hospital in Corpus. I'm really excited to get the catheter taken out, but that means that all of my last chemo treatments will be done through an IV. They can leave the IV in for a couple of days before they have to replace it, so it won't be too bad. Trust me, I would much rather have the IV than have the catheter! It's been nice, but Tubular the Cath, R.I.P. Yup, I named it.

So wish me luck tomorrow! Hopefully everything goes really well tomorrow. They will give me sedation so hopefully I won't feel anything. I can't eat past nine am, so I'm going to stock up tonight! I'll be home tomorrow, but I have to stay at the hospital for two hours after they take the cath out. So that's the latest from Lauren! See you guys soon!!

Love choo all...........
Lauren

P.S. Brenda, the research nurse here at MD Anderson, is having her first baby sometime this week (probably Monday she said). Anyways, we love her. She is the kind of nurse who learned how to communicate with her patients through text messaging and email since technology has taken over the world. She even sends us messages just to say Happy Thanksgiving and Merry Christmas.

I absolutely adore her. Anyways, send up a quick prayer for her and her new baby!

Here's some thoughts....

"Know that it isn't about me, it's about God, He created everything, the stars, the universe, EVERYTHING, and gave everything up to be with us."

"How many times do you make a commitment to Christ? How often do you KEEP it?"

"God knows what you need when you need it."–Unknown

"I am only one, but still I am one. I can't do everything, but I can still do something and because I can't do everything I will not refuse to do the something that I can do."–Edward Everett Hale

"You, O Lord, keep my lamp burning; my God turns my darkness into light." Psalms 18:28 (NIV)

• • • • • • • •

January 18, 2008

Subject: Mid-week update

It's never too late to hope.
Hope is part of our life force.
Never surrender hope.
We know life comes in cycles.
And an upturn can be just around the corner.
Hope helps us struggle through the desperate times.
It guides us through the dark.

So, like I usually do, I pour my little heart out into these emails.
So this one will be no different.

I'm absolutely terrified of this next cycle of chemo. I really shouldn't be, because I've had this same dosage and what not before, but I don't know what the deal is. Maybe it's because I know it will make me sick, or that I no longer have my catheter so *everything* will be done by an IV (and I have to start getting my blood drawn again from good ole regular veins, bummer).

Also, the weather here in Corpus has really changed a lot. We got a major cold front, and it's just rainy and cold out there. I think that has been messing with my sinuses because for the last three to four days I've had a really rough time with a sinus headache, runny nose, and pretty bad cough. No bueno. Last time I went to Houston with a sinus infection, it prolonged my chemo even more. At this point, I want my counts to be good enough to just get this over with! It's *right* there! I'm also worried that we go up there and Dr. Thomas says, "well...go home for another two weeks and get better" or even worse "stay here in Houston, I don't want you to leave" (she's done that before!).

I could just be over panicking about the whole thing, but I mean, you can't blame me! On the bright side, I'm not eating

23857298572 calories a day anymore. My diet is back to normal, no more steroids. Whoo hoo!

Couple prayer requests por favor. My nurse Brenda had her baby on the 15th, a little boy, so hopefully these first few weeks aren't too hard for her! Also, a friend of mine, Becky, is having back surgery today. And my fabulous brother is in Tennessee on a mission trip, so I hope that God works through him this week. Funny story really quick. I bought Eric two cards for the plane rides, and the one that he opened on the way up there was one of those of those music cards that went something like this.

On the front it has a cartoon picture of a girl in a flash dance pose with legwarmers, and it says "You've got the skill, you've got the will..." and then you open it and the song "What a Feeling" comes blaring out of the card! I bet a couple heads turned.

Anyways, I will let you guys know what happens once we get to Houston. We will know a lot more on the 22nd. Keep me in your thoughts and I'll keep you in mine!

Lauren

• • • • • • •

January 23, 2008

Subject: Wrong room, wrong language....and beanie babies.

Oh man. What a trip so far. Let me begin.

We arrived in Houston on Monday night, made good time, got the keys to the hotel room, and took a handful of stuff to the room. We always request a first floor room because sometimes after chemo I have a really hard time walking and what not, and plus it's just way more convenient. So, mom opens the door, looks around and says "this room is not clean." Sure enough, dirty dishes are in the sink, some guy's pillow in the chair, and a newspaper. Ok, so just get the housekeepers to clean it right? Wrong. They left for the day of course. We go tell the front desk, and the only room that they have available is on the third floor. Go figure. And it's not by the elevator. Lots of walking.

Tuesday we head out to good ole MD Anderson, still not sure if I am going to get chemo or not. This past Saturday night I had to go the emergency room because I've been running a fever since Friday night and been having a lot of sinus problems, and Dr. Thomas said I shouldn't have anything going on because I was on two antibiotics. Sooooo we were kind of skeptical about the chemo deal. I get my blood drawn in the morning, hang around and wait for the appointment, the usual thing. We see Dr. Thomas, who decided to put me on a different antibiotic, run more blood work, do a chest x-ray and a CT scan of my sinuses before I start this round, just to make sure it's all ok. That's fine, no biggie. Well, she tells us just to wait in the waiting room to get my blood work (which usually doesn't take long). Of course, the minute we go out there and wait, all of the computers at MD Anderson apparently shut down. Which means no one can do anything! I finally got my blood drawn, which was awful. (sorry if this e-mail is a big complaint!). A few months ago, I was having a CT scan where they shoot iodine into your arm, and it totally

132

messed up that vein in my right arm. It's really painful, but it got a little better and I thought it would be ok to draw blood from it, but I guess not. No blood came from the no longer usable vein. This is the time I really miss my central line.

So this morning they called us at 10:15, told us that we had to be at some radiology center by 11. We get there, and everything goes great. I get my chest x-ray, the CT scan of my sinuses (no IV!) and we are out the door. We got back to the hotel, and the front desk told us that they had a room on the first floor. Yay! As we were driving up, mom had made the comment about one of the windows of the hotel, which was covered in toys, beanie babies, McDonald's prizes, you name it. The whole bottom of the window! I thought it was funny. So mom starts moving stuff to the first floor while I'm upstairs, and when she comes back she says, oh man I hope we didn't make a mistake!

One of the things about this extended stay hotel is that people are here foreeeevvvveeeeeerrrrrr. And it's all kinds of people. You never know what you are going to see! Turns out, beanie baby/toy window room is the room right across from ours. You can hear the kid in the hallway screaming, and then the mom screaming back in some foreign language, and me and mom came to the conclusion that whatever food they are cooking is more than likely some type of road kill. Is that mean? Sorry! It smells *horrible*. I ran around the room spraying body spray and then opened the door and sprayed a ton of it in the hallway. Made us feel better.

AND THEN! (oh I'm not done yet!) The people from MD call us back. This is how the conversation goes.

MD: "Ms. Graham, where are you?"
Me: "In the hotel."
MD: "Well, we need you to come back."
Me: "You've got to be kidding."

133

MD: "Well, Dr. Thomas ordered a chest CT scan too so we need you to come back."
Me: "Ya'll never told us that"
(I'm not being very nice at this point)
MD: "Well, is your mother there? Let me talk to her"
Me: "Whatever."

Turns out, I have to go back to the place, get an IV and get an Iodine injection. I'm sure by now that you all know how much I hate Iodine. It's punishment. Grrr. So, I'm holding off as long as possible to go just because I don't want to, but me and mom are sitting in the hotel room talking about going to Target afterwards to pick out some flameless candles to make at least our room smell pretty. I'll let you know how the rest of the week goes in a few days. If there are no more interruptions, we should be done with this chemo cycle on Valentine's Day. I hope you are all having a wonderful week! I miss you crazy people!

Love choo allllllllllllll
Lauren

"Life is 10 percent what you make it and 90 percent how you take it."–Irving Berlin

• • • • • • • •

January 24, 2008

Subject: Shocker!

Well, don't you know by now that nothing ever goes as planned?

Here is the latest. All of my tests came back normal, no problems with my sinuses, chest x-ray looks good, and most of my blood work is pretty decent. But, my hemoglobin is low (8.0, I think it's usually supposed to be above 9.0), so instead of getting chemo, I'm getting a blood transfusion today (ugh, that means a *big* IV needle. Gross).

Dr. Thomas wants me to be 100% before this next round of chemo, so she is going to wait until next Thursday to start it so I can have another week of antibiotics and start to feel a lot better. So we get to go home!

Yup, that's right Corpus Christi. Watch out, Lauren is coming home! We have to be back next Thursday, but whatever it's ok. I want to see my twin (Eric.) I'm so excited.

Love choooooooo all!!!
Lauren

• • • • • • • •

January 31, 2008

Subject: On the road again....at least to MD Anderson!

Ladies and Gentlemen, the cycle of chemo that was officially supposed to be done today has now officially started today. And it's my grandma's birthday! Somehow, today was going to be special.

As usual, the trip started off with a bang. Guess what room we are staying in? Remember the people I was talking about in my last email with the beanie babies and awful food? That room. And when we walked in, our window was broken. At this point, me and my mom have just learned to laugh at these situations.

I had blood work done this morning and they repeated my chest CT scan. I finally figured out that if I ask the radiology people to slow down the iodine, they will. I have my handy dandy IV in place for chemo (it's in my left hand this time!) and I'm ready to go. Today is a long day. I have that one chemo that is eight hours long. They hydrate you forever before and after, and sometime during this process I have to get a lumbar puncture, which means I have to lay flat for an hour. I'm really going to have to time out my hydrating process! Last week when they ran my chest CT, I had some sort of infection in my chest. Apparently that was some mild form of pneumonia. I had no clue. Duh. Other than that everything is just fine. I'm ready to get this over with finally.

You know that bible verse "I can do all things through Christ who strengthens me?" Well, have you ever taken the time to look at what is written before that Bible verse? Don't worry, I'll show you. It says....

"I have learned to be content whatever the circumstance. I know what it is to be in need, and I know what it is to have plenty. I have learned the secret of being content in any and every situation, whether well fed or hungry, whether living in plenty or in want. I can do all things through Him who gives me strength."–Philippians 4:11-13 (NIV)

So, what's my point? Instead of quitting or pitching a fit to complain, always be content. How do you do that? Look to God for your strength. Bada-bing-bada-boom. Easy. I have found so many times that we have been in situations that are in definite need of some type of complaining or whining, but really, what good is that going to do? All it's going to do is make you feel guilty about complaining and make the person you complained to feel bad. I honestly don't think that there is one human person who is capable of not complaining, even for one day. So try it!

P.S. I'm not saying this because I have some bitterness towards complainers, I just see it all too often here at this hospital and I know I sometimes do it too, so I send these things to you as a reminder to myself also.

Anywho, I'll be sure to send out another update soon.

Love choo allIIIIIIIIIIIIIIIIIIIIIIIIIIIIIIII
Lauren

An oldie but a goodie! I know I've used it before but I'll use it again because I want to.

"If you wake up and don't want to smile,
If it takes just a little while,
Open your eyes and look at the day,
You'll see things in a different way...
–Songwriters: C. McVie/J. McVie; Performed byFleetwood Mac-
"Don't Stop"

• • • • • • •

February 5, 2008

Subject: What do you do with three days of no chemo?

You have a John Travolta marathon of course. I'll get to that in a minute.

So, we went through the first four days of chemo with no problems. Other than slight nausea and being in bed all day, I've been pretty ok. We've gotten out a few times, but as usual, we haven't ventured out much in Houston. I had blood work done this morning and everything is ok. My counts have dropped a little bit, but that was expected. We have our next chemo treatment on Thursday, and our last one is on Sunday. I have a doctor's appointment on Monday, so we decided to just go ahead and stay through the 14th for that weekly chemo. After that, I only have one treatment left in this cycle! Oh man, I'm excited.

That's the latest from Houston! So, what have we been doing? Well, when I'm not sleeping, we watch our TV that has 17 channels but tonight we decided to have a John Travolta marathon! Hairspray, Grease, and Urban Cowboy. If you haven't seen him yet in Hairspray, it's hilarious. I'll be sure to send ya'll another update after we get these next four days of chemo out of the way. I can't wait!

Love choo all......
Lauren

• • • • • • • •

February 11, 2008

Subject: ALMOST DONE!!!

Hey everybody!

whew

So, this cycle of chemo that I was so worried about has been one of the easiest ones so far! I had two lumbar punctures and eight treatments over the past couple of weeks. My counts have dropped a lot. I was only neutropenic for a few days, which is fabulous. I had blood work done on Sunday, and my white count was 1.7, but my platelets were only 26,000. Even though my platelets are low, I'm super excited because that means no Lovenox shots! (at least until I go back to the doctor on Thursday). I've been really lucky because I haven't really had much nausea, but I have been super tired. Other than that, everything has been great.

I also had an appointment with the lady doctor (aka gynecologist) today. We were worried about fertility issues because I didn't get another shot of Lupron (that's the shot that puts me into pre-menopause) and I was still having chemo treatments. Turns out, I can get another dose of the shot. I asked her how long I would have to take it, and she said that since I had chemo once a month for two years, she wasn't sure. I guess it all depends on what my bones can handle and what not. (Apparently the shot causes bone density loss). It's all confusing to me. It's very possible that I could be in pre-menopause for two years. Ugh!

God really is cool. Yesterday, we were up at the hospital and we ran into this woman who was there with her husband. She was asking about my shirt, which said F.A.I.T.H (Fighting Against Illness Through Him) and we had a little conversation about how no one could get through this without God and what not. Later that day, we were eating at Jason's Deli and that woman was there with her husband! We ended up having a nice conversation about how cancer really changes your life and makes you truly appreciate every day and how you can use cancer to bring others closer to God. I think that He plants people like this along the way as encouragers, and I think that is just the coolest thing!

"God doesn't need your capabilities, he needs your availability."

I came across this quote and it got me thinking. I'm constantly telling myself that I need to do this, or I need to learn this Bible story or this Bible verse, on and on and on. Obviously, God gives us talent and it's up to us to use them, but our availability to Him is just as important. Sometimes, instead of constantly talking, we need to just listen. I think that listening to someone is just as effective as talking to them.

We are really excited to get home to everybody on Friday. After that, I only have one chemo treatment (2-21) before I hit maintenance. It's amazing how everything has changed in the past year. I haven't seen my brother or dad since the 31st, which is super hard, especially since Eric is like my twin. I miss them so much! This hotel room gets really old really fast. I'm sad that all of our emails will eventually come to an end (I'm sure ya'll don't want to hear about my everyday normal life!). I can honestly say that writing these emails has encouraged me throughout this whole process and the amount of support that everyone has given me has been amazing. You guys rock! I'll send out another one in a few days.

Love choo allllllll!!!!!!!!!!!!!!!
Lauren

"It's no trick loving somebody at their best. Love is loving them at their worse."–Tom Stoppard

"The busiest person is the one who always has time to help someone else."–Author Unknown

"Prayer, I have discovered, is less about what I say and more about what I hear."–Susan Cosio

• • • • • • • •

February 14, 2008

Subject: Platelet Party! Whooooo hoooooooo!

Heyyyyyyyyyyy folks.

It's me, Lauren. (duh)

Last week when I had blood work done, my platelets were obviously low. Over the past few days, I've had little rashes popping up everywhere (it's not as gross as you think I promise!). They are like, really tiny red dots all over. Don't you know, I named them. Every time a new one pops up, it's like "Hi Spot #98745!" (Sometimes you have to find things that make sense to you and make you laugh even though everyone else thinks you are a complete weirdo). We kind of figured that my platelets were dropping because I'm also bruising a lot. When I had my blood drawn this morning, it wouldn't stop bleeding, and now I have a big ole bruise. Darn it. Sure enough, my platelets are only 6,000. Normal is 150,000-400,000. Ouch.

So today I get a platelet transfusion and two different chemos, the Asparaginase (aka asparagus) and Vincristine. I usually do ok with these two, but Asparaginase is kind of rough. Not looking forward to that. If I have enough energy, me and mom are going to try and go to the Galleria after this. I want some new shoes!

Another big milestone today! I went to MD Anderson without a bandana or hat! That's huge for me. I really dislike my hair at the moment, but it's definitely growing in, with a mind of its own. Mom thinks it is going to be curly, but we will see!

Love choo all!
Lauren

oh ya....

Happy Valentine's Day!

• • • • • • •

February 23, 2008

Subject: I'M DONE!!!!

Hey everyone! It's me!

It's been an interesting last few weeks, so I'm here to update everyone!

First of all, I am officially done with this chemo crud. I'm in maintenance now! For those who forget (like me), maintenance means a lumbar puncture once every three months and only one dose of chemo every month for two years. No biggie, that's nothing! I'm super excited to have this done and over with. Hopefully life will return to normal! It's going to be nice to wake up in the morning and not be sick because of chemo! Whoo-hoo!

Our last dose was on Thursday, and we decided to fly out there because it was just a quick visit. Of course our plane coming home gets cancelled due to weather. We should have known not to make any plans because nothing ever works out the way we expect it too! Thank God for nice people who let us stay at their house! We made it home Friday morning and slept in this morning and it was glorious!

So what now? I have to have blood work done twice this week and then again before we go back to Houston. We go back on March 11 for blood work, chemo, lumbar puncture and a bone marrow aspiration. Grrr. We scheduled the BMA with sedation again, so I'll be sure to let you know if it works this time! The party is still on for March 29. I'll be sending out invites later on, soon I promise! Anyways, I'm sure that I am forgetting something in this e-mail, but I'm starving and I really want to go eat something! More later!

Love choo allllllll
Lauren

• • • • • • •

Sunday, March 2, 2008

Subject: Invites

Here we go!

40+ chemo treatments............................$200,000
8 hospitalizations.......................................$250,000
11 E.R. visits..$35,000
10 blood transfusions $10,000
Being cancer free ....PRICELESS!!!!

OH YA We are having a PAR-TAY!

March 29, 2008
3:00pm-9:00pm

I miss everyone so much, and I would love to see as many of you as I can. You don't have to stay the whole time, you can come by for 15 minutes or an hour, whatever you feel like! Please let me know if you plan on stopping by though so that we can have some idea of how many people to expect. I hope to see you there!

Love choo all!!
Lauren

• • • • • • •

March 12, 2008

Subject: I never promised you a rose garden..........

Oh goodness. Yesterday is defiantly worthy of an email.

So, I've been sick for a while (since around the 24th of February). First, it was just a lot of nausea and a lot of sleeping. Within the past couple of days the nausea isn't quite as bad, but I've developed a super runny nose and a cough. We went to the ER on Saturday, and they did a chest x-ray and an EKG and some other blood tests, but everything came back normal. They gave me two bags of fluid, and I started to feel a little bit better.

We left to Houston on Monday because we were scheduled to have a bone marrow aspiration, chemo and lumbar puncture on Tuesday. I've learned to never make plans at MD Anderson because the chances of your day going as planned is usually not going to happen. Let me tell you about my day.

I always joke around with people and say I have a "Top Five" list, like "Top Five Most Embarrassing Moments" or "Top Five Stupidest Things You Have Ever Done". Yesterday was definitely in my top five "Worst Days Ever."

We started the day with blood work (around 6:45 in the morning). I already wasn't feeling great because I hadn't eaten anything (I couldn't eat because I was having sedation with my bone marrow aspiration). When they drew my blood, I felt like I was going to pass out and it was just not a fun experience. When we went to go ask for a schedule, I made everyone's day by throwing up in the hallway. Glorious.

You know that you are having a bad day when the best part of your day is the bone marrow aspiration, simply because they completely sedated me. It was the best ten minutes ever! I felt a little bit better after that, but not for long. Dr. Thomas decided to skip out on chemo yesterday and instead she ordered a whole bunch of tests. I was already having bad luck with needles, so when they tried to start an IV for my sedation, the first one didn't work and the second one that they placed is in my hand. My veins in my arms are super sensitive, and the needle that they placed in my hand was too small for the CT scan injection, so they had to put a bigger needle in the most sensitive vein in my whole arm. I asked her not to, but she said it was the only place they would put it.

Needless to say, at this point I'm *thrilled*.

We went on to get an EKG (no biggie), and echocardiogram (which hurt because they shove this little ultrasound stick into your chest) and my favorite, the CT scan. Most of you know that a while back, I had a bad experience with the scan because the iodine injection messed up my vein because it got pushed so fast. Ever since then, they say that as long as I ask the technician to administer it slowly, it shouldn't be a problem. Well, I asked her, and she said she couldn't because they were looking for blood clots, so it had to go fast. What?!?

So, our three day trip has turned into a five day trip. Sean's birthday is tomorrow, so I'm super bummed because I will miss it. I'm hooked up to this 48 hour pump that is constantly giving me fluids and nausea medicine. The bag of fluids is like as big as my whole body! I get to carry it around everywhere (not that I'm going many places!)

The party is still scheduled for the 29th. I know that some of you haven't gotten that email yet because so many of you get these emails from other people who forward them, but we are waiting for another week or so just to make sure. It's very possible that it could be postponed for a few weeks. I want to be well enough to see everyone! I'll keep you posted and let you know how everything is going!

I love choo allllllll
Lauren

• • • • • • • •

March 18, 2008

Subject: So you had a bad day....

Hey everyone.

Just a quick update here. First of all, the party is postponed until further notice. I'm thinking one of the last two weekends of April, but I'm not entirely sure just yet. Don't worry, I will let you know!

Secondly, we just got back from the ER. Around 5:00 p.m., my stomach started to really hurt, and I couldn't keep any food down. Then around 9, I started to have back spasms again. No bueno. We went to the ER around 11:30 and they gave me a bag of fluids and lots of pain and nausea medicine through an IV. They didn't get it on the first try, so I had to get poked twice.

With the exception of today, I've been doing a lot better. I'm probably over-doing myself, but it's so hard not to when you feel good for the first time in a long time. Keep me in your prayers. I may be cancer-free, but I am still going through so many struggles health wise. I just can't seem to get better!

Love choooo all
Lauren

• • • • • • •

March 29, 2008

Subject: I'm back!

Hello everyone!

Needless to say, it's been an interesting week. Everything worked out great at the hospital on Tuesday, and I was able to get my lumbar puncture and chemo. We even had enough energy to go to the Galleria afterwards! It's been a good week to hang out with my friends and family, and I'm looking forward to spending the rest of the day with them. On Thursday I went up to TAMU-CC (my college) and met with the disabilities office and got all of the paperwork that I need to get filled out, and next week I have a meeting with my advisor to see if everything will work out with what I want to do! The entire car ride up to Houston was spent looking through the TAMU-CC catalog, trying to figure out what direction to go here so I can graduate. I'm still going to major in communication. I could seriously be a summer camp counselor for the rest of my life, that would be so sweetastic, but I figure I need to look into some form of a "real" job.

Here are some of the upcoming medical deals. Early next week I go in to get my shot of Lupron to throw me back into pre-menopause (*Hello* hot flashes!). I have to go back to Houston in early May to get a bone density scan to make sure that my bones can handle the shot. Also, my next round of IV chemo is scheduled on April 22 in Houston. We got a few new medications while we were there in Houston. I'm on steroids (again), but this time it is only for five days a month. I also have to take two chemo pills a day (no biggie) for the next two years, and once a week I have to take twelve chemo pills all at once. We haven't tried that one out yet, so we will see what happens. After my last ER visit, Dr. Thomas thinks that I have just dealt with some type of upper-GI problem for a long time, and all the medication I guess sends it into overdrive, so I'm also on a nausea medicine around the clock to try and keep it under control. Ok, I think I got all of that right, but who knows!

I keep finding these quotes/cheesy inspirational things that I can't get out of my mind, and I usually throw them into e-mails, but since I haven't been writing as much I just don't know what to do with myself!

As a cancer patient, I have learned:
*Don't wait until rough times to develop your relationship with God, family and friends.
*It's ok to ask God questions, but not okay to demand answers.
*Cancer respects no one, rich or poor.
*Living isn't always easy, accepting that fact makes it easier.
*It is impossible to live our tomorrows today.
*Faith is for the unknown, not the known.
*No trial comes without lessons and assignments. What I choose to do with them is up to me.
*God is faithful.
*Cancer is a coward, it doesn't fight fair and I must be ever-vigilant against its return.
*As long as there is breath and God, there is hope!
*We are God's PERSONAL touch to other hurting people.
–Rachel Bailey

Also, I have learned that despite this battle you deal with everyday, you still have bad days, and you still have good days. Obviously, there are worse days than others, but on those days you have to sit there and realize that there are other people in this world that are going through something way worse than you can possibly imagine. So when you pray in the morning or night or whenever, remember those people, no matter how bad your day is. It helps me.

So, with that said, I believe I am done rambling. And yes, the party is still on. I really want to make sure I am well for it, and May 3 is looking to be a better date. It doesn't run into chemo or finals, so we are shooting for that date. I'll definitely send something out soon, so don't worry!

I love choo alll!!!!
Lauren

Enjoy the quotes!

"Tell the negative committee that meets in your head to sit down and shut up."–Kathy Kendall

"Laughter is an essential amino acid."–Patch Adams

"I don't look at what I've lost, I look at instead what I have left."
–Betty Ford

"Don't avoid me just because I am ill. Be the friend, the loved one, you've always been. Weep with me when I weep. Laugh with me when I laugh. Don't be afraid to share things with me. Call me first, but don't be afraid to visit. I need you, I get lonely. Bring me a positive attitude - it's catching! Help me celebrate today, tomorrow - life!"–Estelle Caputo

"Do you know what a winner is? Somebody who has given their best effort, who has tried the hardest they possibly can, who has utilized every ounce of energy and strength within them to accomplish something. It doesn't mean that they accomplished or failed, it means that they've given it their best shot. That's a winner."–Walter Payton

• • • • • • • •

April 5, 2008

Subject: My wonderful evening

I had a fabulous time tonight I totally want to share it with everyone. I know that lately I've been super fussy, just because things haven't been going the way that I intended them to, and it's just been a weird week.

I had blood work done last week, and everything came back normal. My white count was way high (6.9), it's usually one or something! The only downside of that is that it caused major bone and muscle pain all week. Hopefully this is the last time that I have to go through it! I also started physical therapy. They do their little assessment to see what your limits are and what not, and while she was checking out my back, it became very apparent very quickly that my back is all sorts of messed up. I've been having a lot of back pain, and apparently the muscles that are around my spine are not working the way they are supposed to. Go figure. Other than that, I've been doing ok physically. I haven't really gotten out much though just because I haven't felt good.

Anyways, I'm writing this e-mail because I am so just on cloud nine right now. I've been really interested in Relay for Life lately, and TAMU-CC was holding the event there on campus so I went with a few of my friends to kind of check it out. For those of you who don't know, Relay for Life is a fundraiser that helps raise money for cancer by having teams walk around a track all night long and just find ways to raise money. They start the walk off by having all of the survivors walk around the track with their teams behind them and then you have a member of your team walk throughout the night. Anyways, they all had these neat "Survivor" sashes, and my super awesome friends found the people who were in charge and got me one of those super cool sashes! And not only did I get the sash, but I got a whole goodie bag of "cancer" toys, a shirt, pen, book....just a lot of really neat things.

Your friends can buy you a bag and decorate it to honor those who lose their battle and those who overcome it. Anyways, they have this neat little ceremony where they talk about the importance of those who go through cancer, and they turn all of the lights off, light a glow stick in the bag, and everyone walks around the track to honor these people. Miss Molly made me one of these super cool bags! And all the girls signed it! So we found the bag, and went through the little ceremony, and then we all walked around the track. It meant so much to me because this was one of the first times I was able to be a part of something that my friends and family were doing in honor of me. It always means a lot to have someone honor you, but I can't put into words what it means to have your family and friends telling you how much they love you and how meaningful you are, all because of this thing called cancer. I know it doesn't sound that impactful in an e-mail, but I was truly honored to be a part of this tonight. I love my friends!

I love choo alll!!!!!!
Lauren

"I shall pass through this world but twice-once before cancer and once after cancer. Let the 'after' be the most treasured."–Author Unknown

• • • • • • • •

April 14, 2008

Subject: You know, just go with the flow.....

Hola mis amigos!

Well, once again it's been an interesting last couple of weeks (do I ever have un-interesting weeks?). Let's get started shall we?

Medically speaking, I'm doing ok. No ER visits since St. Patrick's day, so go us! Every so often I'll have a day where I physically just don't want to do anything because my back hurts or whatever, but everyone has days like that! I started physical therapy three times a week. I'm doing a gajamillion times better that I was that first day, and hopefully within a few more weeks I will have some of my strength up.

Physically/emotionally, I could be a lot better. But once again, I've just gotten to the point to where I have to wake up each day and just tell myself, ok Lauren, there's nothing you can really do, so put on your big girl britches and just deal with it. I'm having a hard time with the weight gain (twenty pounds! sick!). Please, I understand that yes, I should just be grateful to be alive and well and what not, but I was a girl before all of this happened, so yes, I can be vain about my looks if I want to. It's very hard to walk past a mirror and have an image of what you used to look like in your mind and see something completely different. Also, my hair grew back in with a vengeance, but I think at this point it's a stand still. It's just kind of chilling out saying, nope, I don't think I want to grow anymore right now.

.....but I want you to grow!

I did get a new wig that looks spectacular (red!), or at least I think so. I was telling my grandma the other day, long hair is kind of just like my security blanket, so I just feel better when I have it! And yes, me and Sean aren't dating anymore. I'm getting a lot of questions about that one too. Just know that we decided that this whole process is a lot to handle and it's hard to build a relationship when you are trying to focus on other things, so no more dating for now. Any major illness can be a huge stressor when you are trying to build a foundation for a relationship, and I completely understand that we are just overwhelmed with trying to make it grow and maintain things. That's the end of that and I really don't want to talk about it. Was much much harder than I ever expected it to be.

So, with all of that said, who in the world do you rely on when things just aren't going your way? I know. Eric Graham, that's who. That kid is hilarious!

Love choo all!
Lauren

• • • • • • •

May 2, 2008

Subject: Why hello!

Hey everybody!

Long time no update. Everything is still pretty much the same, but I'll update you anyways!

It's been a month since I started physical therapy, and it's going really well! I'm slowly but surely getting better each day, so I'm excited about it! I had my evaluation today and everything has improved a lot! This past week was really hard though, because the steroids that I'm on cause a lot of bone pain. Therefore, physical therapy was torture! My counts aren't recovering like I want them too, so that's kind of a bummer. It's taking a lot longer than I thought. They have already had to cut my chemo dose in half because my counts were just dropping like nobody's business. Hopefully they can figure out what doses work for me soon!

I'm still dealing with the weight gain. I know, I know, I keep talking about it, but come on! It's hard when you put on twenty pounds in a couple of months! I need to go to Fast Food anonymous. It's getting ridiculous. So, I have decided that I will attempt to eat healthy (how many times have I said this?). We went to HEB tonight, bought a whole bunch of veggies and what not and actually cut them up and put them into Ziploc bags. Except on my bags, I wrote things like Whataburger, Taco Bell, and ice cream. So, the goal is to eat healthy, or something like that. I'm trying to cut back on the sodas too, which is going to be hard, because I *love* my Dr. Pepper. But oh well juices are going to have to work for a while. Lauren needs to drop a few pounds. It's really sad when you have to buy new pajama pants because even those are too tight.

I hope you are all excited for the party! (MAY 10!!) I'm so excited! It's going to be so much fun, and I can't wait to see everyone there.

Love chooooooo all!!!!!!!
Lauren

"Learning to laugh at trouble radically increases the amount of things there are to laugh at."–Author Unknown

• • • • • • • •

May 29, 2008

Subject: Whole year?!

Well folks....

It's time for an update. Can you believe that it has been a whole year since I was diagnosed with the big "C"? It amazes me how much your life can change in one year. If you would have told me a year ago that I would be sitting here writing about the things that I do, I would have said "you crazy!" I've learned so much and I figured ya'll would like an update as well.

Things have been going pretty well! Both the Corpus and Austin parties went awesome, and it was really cool to put names to faces. I had my monthly IV chemo last Wednesday. It went ok, but it definitely wiped me out. I had stopped taken the oral chemo for a while because my counts kept dropping, so the combo of starting IV and pills again kind of took it all out of me. We spent the weekend in Austin and I was able to see my "sister" graduate from pre-school. She's all grown up! It was a blast!

I'm still in physical therapy. In fact, today we decided that instead of going on to the next step, I'll go ahead and have another four weeks of actually PT. I'm mentally ready to go back to work, but I don't think I can physically handle it yet. I've been getting super wiped out the last week or so really easily. It's hard for me because I finally start to feel good, but then I don't feel good for one day and it all goes downhill. Bummer. Got to keep high spirits though!

I've learned this past year that *anything* can happen. You truly find out who your friends are and what they mean to you. I while back, I sent out an e-mail called "What Cancer Cannot Do" by Bob Gotti. Here it is again, just slightly re-vamped.

It cannot shatter Hope - "God does not always take us out of problematic situations, but He gives us the peace we seek as we proceed prayerfully through each experience."–H. Norman Wright

It cannot corrode Faith - "Unless the LORD had given me help, I would soon have dwelt in the silence of death. When I said, 'my foot is slipping,' your love, O Lord, supported me. When anxiety was great within me, your consolation brought joy to my soul." Psalm 94:17-19 (NIV)

It cannot cripple Love - There's a line from a song I love, it says this. "You can love someone with all your heart, for all the right reasons, when tomorrow they can choose to walk away...love them anyway."–Martina McBride. I honestly believe it is better to have experienced love and lost it than to not have at all.

It cannot kill friendship - One thing I have definitely learned in the past year is that your true friends come about when you need them too. I've had so many people who weren't able to deal with cancer or the things that come along with it, so it makes me that much more grateful for those who have stuck by me.

It cannot suppress Memories - "We are not primarily put on this earth to see through one another, but to see one another through."–Peter DeVries

It cannot invade the Soul - You can be bitter or upset with everything that has happened, or you can THANK GOD that you are still alive. Think about that one.

It cannot steal eternal life - I still know where I am going.

It cannot conquer the spirit. - Even on the days when you feel like everything is going wrong and you don't want to get out of bed, remember that cancer won't break down your spirit. It's up to me and those around me to keep up the positive attitude.

I know it isn't much, but it is somewhat of an update. Hope everyone is well!

Love choo allllllllll
Lauren

• • • • • • • •

June 16, 2008

Subject: Saka J. Wea and more!

Hey everyone!

It's been a while since I sent out an e-mail, and I'm in an e-mailing kind of mood, so aren't ya'll lucky? Lots has happened, hope you are interested, here we go!

Ok, so the biggest thing that has happened recently is that I was able to go to camp! The same camp that I wasn't able to go to last year, I was able to go and be a sponsor and it was amazing. I was really worried the first day because it was so hot and I wasn't sure if I was going to be able to make it through the camp, but God helped me out. I kept thinking of the footprints story, and how God carried the man when there was only one set of footprints, and I feel like a lot of the time this past week, God was walking through me, if that makes sense! We had a golf cart that was decked out in Hawaiian gear, including inflatable flamingos and monkeys and Hawaiian plate hub caps equipped with lights. Oh ya, it's as funny as it sounds. We had one girl accept Christ and she was baptized on Sunday so it was just overall an amazing camp! We also had a lot of fun coming up with new names for our name tags. Here are a few examples! Saka J. Wea, Bay B. Mawma, Rawmen Noo Dle, Rob O. Tussin, Tear E. Aki.....you get the idea. Then we turned in the name tags and said they were "lost" so that they would announce it during lunch. Good times.

I've been struggling a lot lately with holding grudges against people, and I've realized that I am having a really hard time letting things go. I was talking to the camp pastor about this, and how I feel like I am never going to be able to shed this "cancer" skin. I feel like people just look at me and the first thing that comes to their mind is the whole cancer issue. Bummer huh? I came to realize that I really need to use these next few years to glorify

161

what God has given me. In fifteen years, cancer will just be a part of my past, just a little blip. I don't know if that has any relevance whatsoever, but it's just been bugging me! I really have to set my priorities straight, and just learn to let go of the things in the past.

Medically, well. Blah. They scheduled my chemo on the 17th, and I had a bit of an argument with the people at MD. In case you don't remember, my birthday is the 19th, and I definitely want to be on top of my game for that! No chemo for me! I begged and begged, so they moved it to the 24th. I'm getting a triple whammy. How exciting! I start the morning off with blood work, then a bone marrow aspiration with sedation thank Jesus, then a doctor's appointment, a lumbar puncture, and chemo. Lovely. So look forward to another e-mail in a week or so about how that went. I'm still struggling with the weight gain thing, but I'm getting used to it. A lady at our church didn't even know who I was, fun huh? I have to start the steroids again on the 24th also, so I know to expect a lot of bone pain. Please pray that I will prepare myself mentally and physically for it. Lots of painkillers and heating pads for a week or so.

Anyways, how is everyone? I love hearing back from you, so let me know!!

Love choo all!
Lauren

• • • • • • • •

June 25, 2008

Subject: My Little Guppy

Hey everyone!

Thanks for all the birthday wishes! I had an awesome time and I do believe that Catchphrase is on the Top Ten list of coolest inventions ever.

Well, we survived another trip to Houston. First things first, all of my tests came back and everything looks great. Now on to the fun stuff.

We arrived at the hospital on Tuesday around 7:30am for blood work. That's completely normal. From there we went on to the outpatient surgery, so I could get some lovely cocktail of who knows what to put me out for the ten minutes of my bone marrow biopsy. A few days before, I went bowling with Eric and our friend Meagan. You know how a lot of places have those super cheesy stick on tattoos? This screamed "opportunity". So, while we were waiting for the bone marrow biopsy, I put on two of these fake tattoos, one of Donald Duck and one of Winnie the Pooh. I didn't say anything when then lifted up my shirt and saw the tattoos, I just waited for them to say something. Realizing that they weren't, I spoke up right as the medicine started to kick in and said, "hey, you know those are fake right?". Everyone started laughing and Brooke, our cool PA said, "Great! I was getting worried!"

So, afterwards, I was super duper sleepy and slept off all the medication in the patient care facility. My mom had brought me back some chicken nuggets, and of course, I insist on opening like every single packet of ketchup before I eat anything, which I'm sure was funny to watch because not only was I half asleep, I still felt like I swimming in that medicine. The tubing that they had used on my IV was seriously like 6 miles long (way bigger than usual) and in my clouded state I couldn't really control where that thing was going to land and sure enough....bloop...there goes my IV into my champion pool of ketchup. My mom missed this whole event, but the guy sitting across from me started to laugh and told me to just make sure I cleaned it off! I guess you can say that I truly am Popeye's granddaughter now - ketchup runs in my veins! (For those of you who don't know my grandfather, he is a ketchup-aholic. No joke.)

Then we see Dr. Thomas, one of our PAs, and Brenda and everything is going just fine and dandy. Don't you know that there is never really a "good" day at MD Anderson? We didn't get called back for our appointment until around 3:00 pm, which is pretty late considering we usually are called in right around lunch time. Once we signed into the clinic, we waiting about another hour or so to be called back into the room. The nurses started me up on some Ativan to help calm me down (you would want it too if you were fixing to have a needle shoved in your back! Ok, maybe not "shoved", but you get my point). Finally around 6:00 pm or so Brooke came in to do my lumbar puncture. I felt kind of bad because it was already late in the day, but seriously, I don't want lumbar punctures from anyone else! She is fast and gets to the point and makes it as painless as possible. Anyways, after the lumbar puncture, the nurse's started to act like I was finished other than laying flat for an hour, um....I still need the IV drip chemo! The nurse said that she hadn't gotten any orders for it, but she would go look. About two hours later, she shows up, says that they can't find the orders and there isn't anything that can be done at this point because Dr. Thomas had already left for the day. This is where frustration began to set in!

Realizing that we really had no option but to come back in the morning, I asked the nurse if I could keep my IV in so that they wouldn't have to start a new one. By the way, the chemo totally messes with your veins. My once juicy, amazing, wonderful veins are now the equivalent of dried up spaghetti noodles. I have one good vein that I use for my weekly blood work, his name is Guppy. Ok anyways moving on. The nurse said that was fine and shouldn't be a problem, they would just use my IV in the morning. She comes back in with a schedule, and our appointment is as 12:00 pm. GRRR!

So, we wake up this morning (Wednesday), called the charge nurse and asked if we could just squeeze in or if we would still have to wait the average hour or so wait to be seen. She said that they were extremely busy and there were thirteen patients ahead of me and blahblahblah, ok, anyways, I got transferred to a different unit. When I got up there, the first thing the nurse tells me is, "Oh no, we can't use that IV." No, "Hi, how ya doin' ". Jeez. I felt really bad because I snapped at her so if you can hear me nurse....I'm sorry. I wouldn't have been so angry if they would have just taken the IV out the night before, it's not fun to sleep with one! I ended up having to get a new IV in my forearm (pretty painful but better than my hand), and we finally got out of there around 2:45.

Once again, I am so grateful that I am able to be humorous with this situation. Today in the chemo ward, I was kind of startled to see so many people looked just plain ole mad. I don't blame them. I really do believe though that you have to be funny about it and see God's grace through it all.

So, those are my MD Anderson shenanigans for this month. I go back in September for another bone marrow and lumbar puncture. I can not wait to see what thrills await me. Until then folks, peace out!

Love choo allllllllll!!!!!!!!!!!!!!!!!!!!!!
Lauren

• • • • • • •

August 8, 2008

Subject: Ice Ice Baby and an exercise ball. That's right.

Hey everybody!

It's been a long time since I have sent out an update so here we go!

Medically, everything is going great. I have figured out the cycle of this crazy chemo! I get the chemo done and I feel kind of crummy for about a week, and then the day I stop taking the steroids all my bone marrow goes into overdrive and I start getting the bone pain. Bummer, I know, but we are starting to finally figure out different ways to keep the pain at bay. Lots of Motrin and painkillers! I'm still really stiff every day, so I'm working on stretching my muscles more, and sometimes when I am walking or dancing my bones kind of give out. Other than that, I'm doing great! I still struggle with the stupid weight gain, but I'm slowly starting to realize that this is going to be a very long battle and I better try to get used to it the best that I can.

I start school on August 27, so I am really excited about that. I am taking psychology, media and society, interpersonal communications and drug use and abuse. It's going to be a fun semester, I think! As far as my job is concerned, I did go back and work a few shifts, but physically I'm just not ready to wait tables yet. It's kind of a bummer, because it is such easy money, but I just can't do it yet. So, I'm going to start working with a temporary agency with the help of a friend of mine. We will see how that goes!

Ok, I know I am harassing you people about Relay for Life, but come on! It's like, consuming my life! So far, we have raised $1255! How cool is that!? My original goal was $100, so we have come a long way. The relay is on August 15 here in Corpus, so anyone is welcome to come and join us out there. For those of you who haven't donated but are thinking about it, just do it! My goal is to stay in the top five, and these other people are starting to catch up! Let me know if you would like to come out there on Friday, I would love to see you! Also, I need some fundraising ideas for while we are there.

And last but not least, I leave you with some new YouTube videos that we made last night. The first one is a dance video me and Eric made to "Ice, Ice, Baby" and the second one is Eric and Meesha rolling down the hallway with an exercise ball. (Grace, I promise I did not come up with this one. Those two great minds did it all by themselves). I hope you enjoy them!! Have a great day!

I love choo allllllllll!!!!!!
Lauren

• • • • • • • •

August 20, 2008

Subject: Way to meet a goal people!

Hey everybody!

Been awhile since an update! First of all, thank you so much to everyone who donated money for Relay for Life. It was our first time to go out there and really participate, and we all had a blast. Our final total was $1525! How awesome is that? I'm really excited because I was able to stay in the top five, which was my ultimate goal. The crazy thing is that when I started, I wasn't even sure if I would be able to make the $100 minimum! We are definitely going to do this again next year! We started with the survivor walk, which was really awesome because I was able to walk it with my nurse who helped me so much here in Corpus. Walking that walk with all those other people who have been through the same things that you have...I'm at a loss for words. No one has to say anything, it is just understood that we all support each other and we all understand. The entire track was lined with lumenarias, and it was inspiring to see all the different decorations that people had made. We even managed to get ourselves in the paper!

I had chemo yesterday, so we are down to 18 treatments! Everything went fine. My biggest complaint is that the more and more treatment that I am getting, the harder and harder it is for the nurses to find a vein to work with. Six months ago, it was no problem, but now it usually takes them a good five to ten minutes of slapping my arm around to find one! Oh well. We will see what happens with that one.

School starts next Wednesday, so keep that in your prayers! I am so excited about it! We went and bought books a few days ago, and I'm all set with the Disabilities office. Please keep me posted with how ya'll are doing. I know these e-mails don't get sent out quite as often as they did before, but I still think about all of you, all the time!

Love choo allllllll
Lauren

• • • • • • • •

Lauren was asked to be the spokesperson for our local NBC Affiliate for the National "Stand Up to Cancer" program. There was only one break in programming throughout the telecast; it showed pictures of Lauren pre and post cancer treatment, and she read this speech that she wrote.

September 7, 2008 Stand Up to Cancer

My name is Lauren Graham. I am a 22-year old Texas A&M University-Corpus Christi student majoring in Communication, and I am a cancer survivor. I was diagnosed with cancer in May of 2007, and I have learned more in the past year than I could have ever possibly imagined. My entire life was turned completely upside down in a matter of weeks. Other than a few swollen lymph nodes, I appeared to be completely healthy. I was a full time student and I worked a part time job at a local restaurant, so I was constantly busy. One swollen lymph node turned into eleven, and after a biopsy of two lymph nodes I was officially diagnosed with T-Cell Acute Lymphoblastic Lymphoma. My family and I were sent to MD Anderson in Houston, and after more testing, the doctors discovered that I also had Leukemia. 33% of the cells in my bone marrow were cancerous. I immediately started a heavy regimen of chemotherapy and within a few weeks I was in remission. I still had to go through several months of chemotherapy, and I will continue to do so for the next eighteen months. I knew from the beginning of this process that I wanted to become involved any way that I could, and the American Cancer Society gave me that opportunity.

There are so many reasons to take a stand against cancer. First of all, I feel that people should have something to look forward to. I know that a lot of people feel that cancer is some kind of death sentence. In reality, it is a new lease on life. You become a part of a club that no one ever imagines they will be a part of, and you get the opportunity to spread awareness about something that will change people's lives. It is ultimately your decision how you will face this, and I think that every bit of positive outlook helps. Everyone is affected by cancer at some point, and that is why I feel no one can go untouched by this disease. Our local American Cancer Society has done so many things to help cancer patients, and I never knew about any of these things until I became a patient myself. I believe that a huge part of a patients healing process begins with attitude. Cancer can be devastating, not only mentally but physically as well, especially to women who have to deal with hair loss. Our cancer society donates wigs to patients, and also offers a Look Good, Feel Better class that teaches patients how to mask certain cancer features along with donating make-up. Little things like this can have such an impact. I still have pictures from the day that I went to try on many different wigs with my family.

The American Cancer Society has helped me maintain that positive attitude throughout this ordeal. The staff is always friendly, and they know what you are going through. It is a huge relief to know that you are not going through this process alone, and it is refreshing to see that these people have made it through. It encouraged me to keep fighting and to keep going. If they could do it, so could I! Even though they have no idea who you are, they are not going to judge you, but they instead are going to open their doors with loving arms. In the beginning, I definitely felt lost in this big cancer world, but after talking to more and more people at the Cancer Society and seeing different ways that I could get plugged in, I started to feel better about myself.

People need something to believe in. Patients need to believe in themselves. We all need to realize how important it is to never give up in the fight against cancer. I never want my children to hear those words, but I know that if they do, the American Cancer Society will support not only me, but everyone who has been in my path before, who is in it now, and who will face it in the future. So what do we do? We STAND UP TO CANCER!

• • • • • • • •

September 23, 2008

Subject: Update from the crazy girl!

Hey everybody!

I know it has been a while since I wrote an update, so here we go.

I just had my seven month check-up today at MD Anderson. Everything came back great! There are still 2% of those blast cells in my bone marrow, but everything is still considered to be in remission! So exciting! We started the day off with the bone marrow aspiration this morning, went through the day, and finally got done a while back after the lumbar puncture and chemo. They are having more and more trouble with my veins though. Throughout the day I had to have six different IV's, gross. It's ok though! It's done and over with.

On a personal note, a lot of you have been asking about school. I'm having a blast with it, and I'm really enjoying the classes that I am taking! College gets to be a lot more interesting when you are in classes that interest you! Also, TAMU-CC asked me to be their Survivorship Chair person for the Relay For Life committee! Exciting!

It would be awesome to hear back from all of you! Love you guys!

Lauren

• • • • • • • •

October 27, 2008

Subject: Lauren's lesson of the day!

Hey all!

Here is your monthly update on the wonderful life of Lauren. I had chemo this past Tuesday and everything went fine. They had some trouble with my veins (as usual), but it only took three tries this time! Actually getting the chemo isn't the rough part, it's the after effects of it that are no fun. As much as I hate to admit it, I'm learning that sometimes I need to humble myself and learn when to say no to certain things. You get to a point where you tell yourself that yes you are completely healthy, and yes you can do all these things, when in reality, you need to be really careful and not push yourself so hard. So that is my lesson of the day! Learn that it is ok to sometimes say no if you seriously don't feel like you can do something, whether your mind tells you that you are capable or not. I promise that all made sense in my head!

As far as the bone pain goes, it's kicking in. It's kind of weird, you think you have the pattern down, and then it decides to switch it up on you. Before, it usually would kick in right in the middle of taking the steroids, but the past few months (and this month) it's kicking in after the fact. Bring on the ice packs and Motrin! Also, the problems with my foot are slowly getting better. (Clumsy over here was walking across campus and managed to hurt her foot). I went to the doctor and they gave me a bunch of different options to try, but they think the majority of that pain I'm having is caused by all my other 5000 medications.

School is going really good too, at least I think so! I've been trying a lot more these past few months then I ever did my first three years of college (sorry mom!), but I'm enjoying the stuff that I'm learning this time around, so that always makes a difference. I hope ya'll are all having a fantastic day!

Love choooooooooo all
Lauren

Count your blessings: The best thing about sunny days is that they remind us that gloomy days are only temporary. Take a minute to list 50 things that are great about your life (and the more trouble you have with this exercise, the more you need to do it!) Tuck your list somewhere safe, and refer to it when you need a reminder that a sunny day is just around the corner!

Never forget to look for blessing - even the smallest of joys can brighten the worst of days.–Author Unknown

Think positive whenever you can. When you can't, call someone and have him or her do it for you.–Unknown

• • • • • • • •

November 5, 2008

Subject: Lauren update and what not!

Hey everyone!

Here is the latest update with myself. (If you ever get tired of these, tell me and I'll take you off the mailing list! I know that they are not near as interesting as they were before.) Chemo is working for sure. My white count is down to 3.9. I've been feeling slightly run-down, but nothing more than usual. School is starting to catch up with me but I'm working on it! My next chemo appointment is November 18 (I think) and the next big appointment (the triple whammy, chemo, lumbar puncture and a bone marrow aspiration) is on December 19. So, not looking forward to that, but it's ok! We are down to sixteen treatments! How awesome is that?

This Saturday, there is going to be a big music festival on campus. It's called the Jimmy V festival and all of the proceeds are going towards cancer research. Why do I tell you about this you ask? Because they asked little ole me to be a speaker at this event. Of course I will speak at it! I go on at 7:45 and I have a little ten minute snazzy deal I get to talk about it. If you are interested in coming out to see it, let me know and I will tell you where to go! On the TAMU-CC campus on the Bay Hall Lawn, you should come and check it out!

I miss all of you, and I miss your snazzy emails that let me know how you are doing. Keep me posted friends!

Love choo alllll
Lauren

• • • • • • •

December 18, 2008

Subject: MD Anderson decided to give me an early Christmas present!

Hey everybody!

It's been a while since an update, but there isn't much to report! We are here at MDA today, and I had my bone marrow aspiration this morning, and right now I'm sitting in the waiting room waiting to get my lumbar puncture and chemo. Joy. The bone marrow went really well, and all the results turned out great. My white count is still slightly elevated, so they upping the dosage of one of my medications, nine pills to fourteen! Ugh! Other than that, everything looks really good. Also, I'm getting a flu shot today. I suppose it is for the best, but I still hate shots! My poor veins are hiding out. I have an IV in the weirdest place, in the back of my forearm on my right arm, so it keeps catching on everything.

So, what is my early Christmas present from MDA? I asked Dr. Thomas if today was going to be my last bone marrow aspiration, and she said no, but we would not have to have them every three months. Then I asked her about lumbar punctures, and she said today was the last one! OMIGOODNESS! Those are probably the worst, because at least for the bone marrow I can be completely sedated, not so much for the lumbar punctures. So, no more after today! How exciting is that?

As far as everything else, it's going well. I finished my first semester back to school. I don't think I did as well as I wanted to, but the bottom line is I finished out the semester! My hair is growing back like crazy, and it's finally long enough to be straightened out! Yay! I think I'm finally getting back to normal!

I love you crazy people!
Lauren

• • • • • • •

January 16, 2009

Subject: No Subject!

Hola fellow amigos/amigas!

I've gotten a few e-mails asking how everything is going, so I thought I would send out the big shebackle on the life/health of Lauren for the past month or so. Everything is going ok. Could be better, but it doesn't totally suck, so we are good. I've been battling the awesome cold/cough/flu thing that has been going around, but with my wonderful immune system I can't exactly fight it off like you normal people can. On Tuesday, we went to the doctor here in Corpus and they decided to hold my chemo. It's been awhile since that happened! If you can remember, a normal white blood count is anywhere in the range of 4-11. Mine was 1.8. No bueno. Plus, my liver tests were all out of whack and I was *almost* neutropenic (below that golden 1000 level). What? I thought I was supposed to be back to normal, healthy, whatever you want to call it! They re-scheduled the chemo for yesterday (Thursday), which also just so happened to be the first day of school. Thanks Corpus Christi Cancer people. I survived though! And they only had to stick me one time for the IV!

Having my white count that low kind of threw me for a loop. I wasn't expecting it, and when you hear those low numbers, your mind (well, at least mine) starts to automatically overreact. It tries to think of all the ridiculous reasons why your blood tests are all weirded out. I know that I am technically "cancer free", but I'm definitely still a cancer patient. I was reading a book recently, and it was talking about crossing over from a patient to a survivor. When do you make that leap? Well, the minute you are diagnosed you are not only a patient, you are a survivor of something millions of other people will go through and millions of other people will never have to experience. I kind of came full circle and had a little mini-Lauren epiphany. Yesterday at school, I was thinking to myself, "Am I going to be able to do this? Four classes in one day, a couple of classes I know I am going to struggle with, and work?" I had to sit myself down and think about it. I have fully come to realize that my life will never be "normal". Even though I technically don't look like a cancer patient anymore (if you haven't seen my hair yet, you need to!), I still carry that extra weight on my shoulders that a lot of other people won't ever have to. But it's ok! I'm ok with it!

Sorry, that was a little rambling, but ya'll know me, I do that, a lot. It always makes me feel better. So, guess what? I only have thirteen more months of treatment and I am done! That means only thirteen more stinkin' IV's, 53 more blood draws, and who knows how many pills! I'm so excited! I think we should throw another party at the end of it all, what do you guys think? Right in time for spring break 2010! Ok, ok, I will stop talking now!

I love choo crazy people....
Lauren

P.S. By the way....if you know anyone who is a survivor of cancer, or anyone who was caregiver to someone with cancer, please let me know! I need to start gathering up these wonderful people for Relay for Life! Let me know if you are interested, it's an awesome opportunity. And you get a free shirt. Come on!!

• • • • • • •

January 20, 2009

Subject: What a weekend, I tell you.

Hey folks!

I know, you must be thinking, two e-mail updates from Lauren in like, less than a couple weeks? Just like old times, huh? Well, I was just writing to let you all know about my latest experience with the whole cancer shmancer thing.

So, as you know, I have been doing a little more than I usually do (working a few hours a day, going to school, getting around more), and decided to go shopping with a friend. Well, about halfway up the escalator at Macy's, I started to get extremely clammy, light-headed, and I felt that intense knot of the wonderful back pain starting. Needless to say, I decided my shopping trip was over. Ended up going home, trying all the medications we had here, and right about when it was time to eat dinner, mom was driving me to my home away from home-the Emergency Room.

Ahh, you know, it's been such a long time since I have had to go to the ER. We have a love-hate relationship. 99% of the time, being a cancer patient gets you way bumped up on the list ahead of broken legs, the flu, and whatever else is in there, so that's kind of nice! This time, we walked into the ER about 7:30, and I was in a room by about 7:45, and getting wonderful pain medication by about 8:15. That has got to be some kind of record! The funny thing about this whole situation though....

If you can recall, back when I was having my whole gallbladder episodes, it took a really long time for all of the doctors to figure out what in the world was wrong with me. One doctor in particular thought I just had anxiety and that I was there in the ER for pain medication only, when the whole time it was my gallbladder acting up. Well, I had the same doctor this time and I was treated like a queen! I guess it pays to be nice to people.

Anyways, I'm doing much better now, just still dealing with the after effects of chemo, but it's ok!

I love choo crazy people and thanks for reading all my ramblings, it always makes me feel better.
Lauren

• • • • • • • •

February 23, 2009

Subject: What a weekend!

Hey everyone!

First things first, I've added a lot of new names to my e-mail list, so for some of you this might be your first cancer-shmancer update from me. If you aren't interested, feel free to delete the e-mail or just tell me and I'll take you off the list!

I had my monthly chemo on Friday, but there were a couple of complications. I woke up Friday morning short of breath and with some chest pain. That's scary to begin with, but when you have already had to deal with a blood clot in your lung once, it's even scarier! After chemo, I had to go get a CT scan to see if there were any clots floating around but luckily there wasn't. The downside though is that these last two months have hit me *really* hard as far as the chemo goes. It was getting better for awhile, as far as not being quite so debilitating, but lately it's been hitting pretty much the day after. It feels like someone is giving you a huge bear hug, and squeezing as hard as they can, so you can't breathe! No fun!

So basically, that's the chemo update. And guess what? I only have twelve more IV treatments! How amazing is that? Next month is our three month check-up at MD Anderson, and guess who we have tickets to go see? Keith Urban! (For those of you who don't know, I'm obsessed and have a really cool awesome story from the last time we went to go see him!) Hopefully my backstage pass will work, but since it's the rodeo and not his actual tour, I'm not sure if it will or not.

But anyways, that's the latest! I'm trying really hard to not let this get the best of me, but sometimes it is difficult to keep your spirits up when you are slowly getting used to being "normal" again! I'll send another update when I know more.

I love choo crazy people!
Lauren

• • • • • • • •

March 21, 2009

Subject: Man oh man, what a trip!

Hey everyone!

First things first. Guess who finally met Keith Urban?! MEEEEEEEEE!!!!!!!! Yup, that's right. We finally had the opportunity to use my backstage pass! We completely missed the whole rodeo, but it was totally worth it. My mom and I stood in line for a long time, and they never asked her if she had a pass, she just snuck in with me! We didn't get to talk to him for long, but my mom told him the whole story about how he had met my dad and brother, and how I couldn't use the backstage pass at the last concert because of cancer treatments, and he turns and looks at me and says, "that was you?" I couldn't even speak! He took a picture with us, and gave me an extra hug....ahhhhh I love it.

Anyways, moving on. We saw the pain management doctor, and they upped the dosage on my Lyrica (that's the medication that helps the numbness in my hands and feet), and gave me a different painkiller to see if it will work. Also, Dr. Thomas doesn't want me to take my steroids this time around. She wants to see if that is the true cause of my pain. Hopefully it will all be ok though. My counts were a lot lower than they usually are, and since I'm not taking the steroids this month, I have to be really careful about being around sick people and what not.

Anyways, that is the latest with me! I hope you all enjoy the picture of me and Keith!

love chooooooo all!!
Lauren

• • • • • • • •

April 29, 2009

Subject: Where in the WORLD did these come from?!

"You won't lag behind, because you'll have the speed.
You'll pass the whole gang and you'll soon take the lead.
Wherever you fly, you'll be the best of the best.
Wherever you go, you will top all the rest.
–Dr. Seuss

Hey friends. I've been thinking about that quote a lot for many reasons. 1.) I love Dr. Seuss. Who cares if it's supposed to be for little kids? 2.) The message behind it is so complex yet so easy to understand.

The past few weeks have been *rough*. You get to a certain point in your chemo, and you think, "Ok, I *can* do this"....it begins to develop a routine. But the funny thing about cancer treatment is that it does what it wants to do. The only thing that I can do is try to maintain some type of positive attitude and not let those really rough times get the best of me.

The last few weeks I have had *a lot* of school work to do, and on top of that, we had Relay for Life. Anyways, the weekend of Relay went fine (TAMU-CC raised $24,000!!), but I was just really tired on Sunday and wasn't feeling that great. When I woke up on Monday, I was having chest pains and was kind of on the verge of a nervous breakdown. Ok, now most of you know, but the reason why I get so *freaked* about chest pain is because of the stupid measly little blood clot I had in my lung at one point. Blood clots can be completely fatal, and quickly. So, in my defense, I completely freak out when I get any type of symptom that relates to that. Ok, moving on, so that night, out of nowhere, I started having these crazy panic/anxiety attacks. I would feel this tightness in my chest, almost like when you are trying really hard not to cry, and start breathing all weird and freaking out....gah. It was pathetic.

185

So what do we do? Pack it up and go to the ER. I truly dislike being in the emergency room, but when there is a possibility of dealing with a blood clot, I think it's the best place for me to be. So we go to the ER, wait a few hours, and as soon as I lay down in the room I start getting the panic attacks again. I couldn't breathe right, my hands and feet were all tingly, ugh. Anyways, everything checked out ok and we finally got home in the morning. Once I was asleep, I was fine, but the minute I would wake up, I would freak out all over again. So now I have some handy-dandy anti-anxiety medication in case this happens again. This ER visit took it out of me! I would say at least in the Top Three Worst ER Experiences ever. But it's over, and I'm slowly recovering from it. Some days are better than others.

On the bright side (there is always a bright side!!), I only have ten more stinkin' months of chemo! And Dr. Manalo (my oncologist in Corpus) reduced my lab work, so instead of getting lab work done once every week, I only have to go once every two weeks! Little Guppy just might make it after all!! (That's one of my only veins that still cooperates with me!)

That's the latest update folks. I have chemo again on May 26, and then we go back to Houston sometime in late June to get a full check-up, including a bone marrow aspiration. Gag me. May 28 is my two-year anniversary of being diagnosed. Crazy huh?

Love choooo alll!!!
Lauren

• • • • • • • •

May 27, 2009

...was two years ago tomorrow, and it's also the day that I was diagnosed with cancer.

How crazy is that? Can you believe it's been two years? Two years ago, I was a college student who had no idea what I wanted to do with my life. Two years later, I'm still a college student, have a few ideas about future jobs, but at least I have a degree plan! Two years ago, I was living on my own and paying my own rent with a really good waitressing/bartending job. Two years later, I'm back with the parental units and trying to earn money by acting as a housekeeper for my mom and by working like, four days a month at the hospital. Two years ago, I had happy veins that didn't argue or protest when I occasionally had to get blood work done. Two years later, I only have one vein that works well for blood work, and all my other veins hide whenever it comes to getting an IV. Two years ago, if I didn't feel good, I'd pop some Motrin and be on my way. Two years later, if I don't feel good, I lay in bed all day, sleep on ice packs, and look through the ridiculous amount of medication I have to see if there is anything to make me feel better.

Two years ago, I didn't take any daily medications. Two years later, I think it's a good day when I only have to take about 10 pills instead of 25. Two years ago, I didn't think twice about what to do with my long hair. Two years later, I'm trying to figure out what in the world to do with short, curly hair. Two years ago, I had a wide variety of cute clothes to wear. Two years later, I stick to the same two pairs of pants and four t-shirts since that is all that will fit me. Two years ago, I loved the rain. Two years later, I still love it, but it's bittersweet because of the pain it causes my joints and what not! Two years ago, I only had one really cool battle wound. Two years later, I can't even count how many I have from surgeries and catheters. Two years ago, I had no idea what a PET scan or a bone marrow aspiration was. Two years later, I could tell you what they are and way more. Two years ago, I was counting down the

187

days until my 21st birthday. Two years later, I'm counting down the months until I'm done with treatment. Two years ago, I had a million different friends who I hung out with often. Today, I can count on one hand the number of friends I still hang out with. Two years ago, I didn't know anybody at MD Anderson and had only read about it. Two years later, I can tell you where the Park is, I can tell you that you don't want to be in Infusion Therapy, I can tell you that nothing is ever on time there, I can tell you about the wonderful sleep rooms that they have, I can tell you that every single waiting room has an awesome aquarium in it, and I can tell you that I get excited to see all the staff there, because they remember who you are, they remember your name, and they genuinely act like they care about you.

Ok, so I know that was kind of pointless, but to me it wasn't. So many different things have happened in two years, and I feel like I have had to grow up way too fast. I've had to change a lot of things that I never really wanted to change, and although I'm not happy about how some things have turned out, I wouldn't change it. Cancer has made me a better person mentally, and it has changed the way I look at so many different things. I'm grateful that the past two years have gone by quickly, and I hope that the next nine months go by as quickly as well.

Yup, you heard right. Nine months! (No, I'm not having a baby you weirdos). I am finally in the single digits of how many IV chemo sessions I have left! Ahh only nine more months of all of this craziness. So with hopes that all goes well, I will be finished in March 2010. I can't wait. This past chemo went well. I've been having problems with back pain as usual, so I'm going to go get a chest x-ray after this. Later this week, I have an MRI to try and figure out if I have any nerve damage going on because I keep having nerve-related problems throughout my body. Next month is a big month! We go back to MD Anderson for our three-month check-up, and I have to have a bone-marrow aspiration. Hello sedation! I will be sure to let you know how all of it goes!

Thank you to everyone who has followed my crazy story for the past two years, and thank you for actually being interested in what I have to say. The e-mails kept me going even when I didn't want to, and it always encouraged me to know that other people wanted to know how I was doing. It encouraged me to know that I could make other people laugh, and that I could even help other people who were dealing with crazy issues of their own. I intend on writing these e-mails for the next nine months, maybe not as frequently, but I'll keep you posted.

I love choo alllllll!!!!!!!
Lauren

• • • • • • •

Subject: May 28, 2007....

June 30, 2009

Subject: Chemo....

...is never normal!

One more MD Anderson trip down, only a few more to go! Overall, I have a total of eight treatments left, which means only eight more months! So if all goes well, March 2010 will be my last treatment. Holy Moly I can't wait!

This round of chemo has been particularly tough. Usually what happens is, I'll get the chemo done, and I'll be fine for that day. The next time, I'm slightly wiped out, and by the third or fourth day I'm either slightly functional and moving around or I'm completely knocked down and unable to do anything. Unfortunately, this month was the latter! I felt fine Friday night, kind of laid around on Saturday, and then all day Sunday and Monday I didn't get out of bed at all. It can for sure be frustrating when you have so many different things that you want to do but you can't!

BUT! I can't let cancer get the best of me on these days that I feel awful, I have to maintain that positive attitude, no matter how difficult it is. I'm trying!

Everything came back good with my bone marrow aspiration! No weird crazy cancer cells or anything! I have to have another one soon, but it's ok. Anyways, keep up the encouragement! I know my emails may not be quite as interesting as they were before, it really does help me to open my email and see all those notes of encouragement from you guys!

Love choo all!!!!
Lauren

• • • • • • • •

August 24, 2009

Subject: Inspiration?

Man, you know how you sometimes lie awake at night, just thinking about everything that is going on in your life? If you are like me, you watch TV until 2:00 a.m., usually watching absolutely nothing of importance, then listen to your IPod for another hour and then lay awake even longer just thinking. Do you ever wish there was just a button to shut off your thoughts?

As most of you know, a lot of my medications tend to cause insomnia, which in turn sometimes inspire these lovely emails you people read the next morning. I was listening to my IPod, trying to shut off my brain when this song came on. It's called "I Run For Life" by Melissa Ethridge. The words to this song are just so powerful to me, and every time I hear it I am on the brink of tears because the words scream at me. Lately the whole cancer-shmancer thing has been doing a number on my self-esteem, but ya'll already knew that. Here I am, 23 years old, fixing to start school up again and trying to plug myself into different activities so that I can forget about the fact that I still have to deal with this stuff. I try to cling to the thought that I only have seven months left, but even that sometimes isn't enough. I've been just digging myself deeper and deeper into this shell of a person that I know I'm not, and I know there is only one thing that can bring me out of it. Duh.

I've been asking myself, what inspires me? What am I inspired by? Do people even care what inspires me? Should I even care what other people are inspired by? I need to be re-inspired sometimes, just like everyone else does. Well, listening to this song just reminded me of what God put me on this earth to do. God gave me talents, and I know that one of those talents is being able to connect with people through humor (hey, at least I think so!). So I am going to use that talent to spread awareness of so many things that need to be heard. I've decided. I've always known, but I know that I haven't been as uplifting and positive as I should be lately. God knows what we all need when we need it. I've been screaming that statement in my head over and over and over again, sometimes even arguing with God about it, but of course He always wins. I see people who are in the beginning stages of cancer, and my heart hurts for them. I don't want anyone to ever have to know what that feels like, so I want to spread as much awareness about cancer prevention as possible. I think the biggest numero uno thing is to tell people to *stop smoking*. It's 1) stupid, 2) makes you smell bad, and 3) gives you cancer.

I don't know if there is much of a point to this email, but I'm awake and my mind is going a gajamillion miles a minute so I thought, why not. Here's the latest medical update. We saw the pain management doctor on Tuesday and they said my MRI showed that I do have arthritis in my lower back. I could either get steroid injections (ew) or I could just do lots of physical therapy. I think I'll go for option number two thank you! I'm still battling this cough/cold situation, which isn't good. School starts on Thursday and I'd like to go. My next round of chemo is scheduled for September 9 here in Corpus, and after that session I only have six more. It's getting so close! Thank you for those who are still reading this rambling.

Love choo all crazy people.

Lauren

"If you think you can, you can. If you think you can't, you're right."
–Mary Kay Ash

"Sometimes you don't have everything that you want, but God gives you what you need."

"Anyone then, who knows the good he ought to do and doesn't do it, sins." James 4:17

"I Run For Life"

Songwriter: Melissa Ethridge

It's a blur since they told me about it
How the darkness had taken its toll
And they cut into my skin and they cut into my body
But they will never get a piece of my soul

Hey, I like it. You should too!

• • • • • • • •

October 13, 2009

Subject: Heyyyy!!!!!!

So, this might possibly have been one of the best MD Anderson visits ever in the history of MD Anderson visits.

I had my bone marrow aspiration this morning, and everything went well there. I do forget how much those things hurt though afterwards. It was a few hours before I could walk again, and I'm sure it will be sore for a few more days. I made them put Hello Kitty band-aids on top of the ugly brown band-aid they put on, so at least I have a little fun there.

Our appointment to see Dr. Thomas was around 10:00 am, but I didn't get to see her until about 3:00. It's ok though, it's always worth the wait! So here is the greatest news. As most of you know from previous e-mails, in order for me to be in remission, my blast cells in my bone marrow need to be less than 5%. They usually are sitting pretty around one or two percent, but today my blast cells were at zero percent! I'm so excited! That means no cancer at all! But wait, it gets better (at least to me it does!)

Because of all the flu stuff going around, Dr. Thomas wanted me to have a flu shot. Well, because of the flu shot, I don't have to take my monthly steroids this month! The steroids are what usually cause my bone pain and all my swelling/weight gain. How awesome is that that I don't have to take them this month?! And I don't have to come back here to MDA for another four months instead of three.

We asked her about future treatments and what I will have to do when this is all said and done. After my last IV chemo treatment, I will continue all of my medications for about a month, and then almost all of my meds will be dropped! I'll have to continue to take a couple of them because it's common for patients to develop

194

shingles (weird, I don't get it), so they want to continue a couple of the medications for up to a year. Also, I will only have to come back every six months to check in with Dr. Thomas instead of every three.

So, ladies and gents, I have had over ten bone marrow aspirations. I now have one left.
I've had around 15 lumbar punctures. I have zero left.
I've had around three years of treatment. I have five months left.
I've had over a hundred chemo treatments. I have only five chemo treatments left!

So, if everything goes according to plan, I will be completely done with everything in March 2010. I can't stop smiling! I'm so happy right now it's ridiculous. I hope ya'll's day is as wonderful and fantastic as mine has been!

Love choo all!!
Lauren

• • • • • • •

Subject: Best Visit Ever!

November 21, 2009
Subject: FOUR more!

Hey!

Ok, so here is the latest (for those of you who still read these ridonkulous emails).

I was supposed to have chemo last Wednesday, but my liver counts were too high. Why were they too high? I think it's because I have to take so many medications, and my liver processes them, or something along those lines. My mom has explained it to me multiple times, but I always get distracted when she tells me so I catch bits and pieces. So I was totally bummed that I couldn't have chemo. I know that might sound weird, but at this point, I just want to get on with it! In the beginning I would have loved nine days off, but not now. That's nine days too many if you ask me.

Anyways, I finally had chemo today. I'm crossing my fingers that this round won't be too bad. If you guys remember, last month they told me that I didn't have to take the steroids, but this month I do. The steroids are what cause that crazy bone and muscle pain, so I'm thinking that since last month was kind of easy on the pain scale, this month is going to be horrible. That would be ok normally, but hello! It's Thanksgiving and the last bit of classes for school, so I'm not looking forward to being in some pain during that time. If you see me walking really slow or super stiff, you will know it's because of that!

So if you are keeping count....FOUR MORE LEFT! Four, four, four, that's such a glorious number right now. Two years ago, it seemed like I would never make it to four but here I am! March 2010 is going to be an amazing month, I just know it.

I hope you all have a great Turkey day! By the way, did you know that Thanksgiving is by far my favorite holiday? Well you do now. I'll give ya'll another update as soon as there is something more to tell! I need to go write papers now!

Love choo all!!!
Lauren

• • • • • • •

January 10,2010

Subject: Update

Hey everyone!!

Two super important things to talk about! First, I only have two more treatments after Friday! How awesomely cool is that?! I'll send out another big update in February, I have a visit to MD Anderson then, so I'll know if anything new is up, which there shouldn't be.

Secondly, can you believe it's already time to start fundraising for Relay for Life? If anyone is able to donate anything, it would be so greatly appreciated. The first Relay that I was involved in, I was able to raise over $1000, and I would love to be able to do that again!

Thank ya'll so much, I'll talk to you soon!

Love choo all...
Lauren

• • • • • • • •

February 13, 2010

Subject: Hi there!

Hey everyone!

I haven't sent out an update in awhile, I apologize about that! Here is the latest.

We went to MD Anderson this past Wednesday through Friday to do my second to last chemo treatment. It was actually a pretty decent visit! Eric went with us, so he was just like free entertainment the whole time that we were there. We did blood work in the morning, and then I got to visit with my friend Kristi (she is the one who is the same age as me and got diagnosed with APL three months before I did). We were joking around that it was bound to happen, three years at MD Anderson and we finally managed to get an appointment at the same time on the same day! It was nice to see her! I also got to visit with Brooke (the most super awesomest lumbar puncture lady *ever*, plus she's just cool). We were supposed to meet up with Brenda, but it was raining the entire time we were there so that didn't happen. I think that Dr. Thomas misses me from time to time! When I saw her, I got all kinds of hugs and smiles, which does not normally happen with her.

So after my appointment with her, we met with the pain management doctor, and once I stop taking my meds for chemo, then I can start to wean myself off the pain medication (I don't want to be on it anymore!) So, the way that all that medication shmedication stuff will go, I will have my last chemo sometime in mid-March (smack in the middle of spring break probably!), and then I will continue to take all of my medications for the following month. At the end of that month, I will be able to start stopping the pain medications also. I'm so close!

Chemo went fine. My IV was ridiculous though. Mr. Shaky Hands McGee is the one who started it, so of course it hurt, and it was in the most ridonkulous spot ever, the inside of my wrist. Who does that?

Everything else is going fine with me, just school and gearing up for Relay for Life! (Of course I'm putting the link again in this e-mail so you can donate to a wonderful cause!) I'll send out one more big e-mail after that last chemo to let you guys know how it went, but until then...see ya!

Love choo all!
Lauren

• • • • • • • •

March 12, 2010

Subject: This is surreal

I'm DONE!!

Unbelievable. I can't wrap my head around it After three lonnnnnnnng years of chemo treatments, IV's, bone marrow aspirations, hospital stays, lumbar punctures, ER visits, countless medications, side effects, and who knows what else....I'm *finished*. No more chemo treatments for me!

Who would've thought that when I started these e-mails three years ago that they would become such a huge part of my life? I didn't. I could never say thank you enough to everyone who has constantly supported me with encouraging card, notes, e-mails, etc....I can't even begin to express how much all of those things meant to me. I've kept every card and every e-mail, and whenever I'm kind of upset, reading all these cards always makes me feel better!

Now, on to the main event. This day has been better than I could have ever imagined! My mom wasn't able to go with me to chemo today, so Megan and Meesha (two of my best friends) said they would come and sit with me. They came to Corpus with the party truck, which was just Meesha's truck but decorated. Megan made these awesome party hats that say things like "Freedom" and "she did it," they brought me and my mom flowers, green and orange leis, and a button that says "It's all about me!". My face hurts so much from smiling all day! I don't know why I was blessed with such amazing friends, but I feel so lucky to have these two sisters in my life! They are amazing! They swapped out so one sat with me for the first half of chemo and then one sat with me for the last half. There were pictures being taken as I left the chemo room, and pictures being taken as I was leaving the cancer center. I still can't wrap my head around it!

I have been waiting so long for this day to get here, and now I feel like I can finally close the door on this chapter of my life. Cancer will always be a part of me, but I know that I was given cancer for a reason. I look at this as my blessing in disguise. God has proven time and time again to me that I can't do anything without HIM, and He has rewarded me with so much more than I deserve.

I don't even know what else to say. I'm done. It's finished, I can go on and live my life and just think of this cancer experience as something in my past.

I love choo all more than you could ever possibly know!

Lauren

"Don't stop thinking about tomorrow, don't stop for it will soon be here...It will be better than before, yesterday's gone, yesterday's gone!"

• • • • • • • •

Glossary

Acute Lymphoblastic Lymphoma/Leukemia (ALL) - Cancer of the white blood cells, characterized by excessive lymphoblasts. These malignant, immature white blood cells continuously multiply and are overproduced in the bone marrow. They cause damage and death by crowding out the other normal blood cells in the bone marrow and spreading to other organs. Acute refers to the very short time course of this disease that can be fatal in as little as a few weeks if left untreated.

CT Scan (Catscan) (Computerized Axial Tomography) - a procedure that assists in diagnosing tumors, fractures, bony structures, and infections in the organs by combining many x-ray views with the aid of a computer to provide three dimensional views inside of the body.

Echo (Echocardiogram) - ultrasound or sonogram of the heart which shows two dimensional images of the heart.

John McGovern Health Museum- an interactive science learning center in the heart of the Texas Medical Center in Houston, TX

Locks of Love - Locks of Love is a public non-profit organization that provides hairpieces to financially disadvantaged children in the United States and Canada under age 21 suffering from long-term medical hair loss from any diagnosis by using donated hair to create the highest quality hair prosthetics.

Lovenox - injectable anticoagulant (blood thinner) used to prevent formation of blood clots. Injections are given in the abdomen.

Lumbar Puncture (LP) - also known as a "spinal tap'"- used to remove spinal fluid for testing for cancer cells as well as to inject chemotherapy in order to prevent relapse of the disease into the central nervous system (spine and brain).

MD Anderson Cancer Center - #1 Recognized cancer center by US News and World Report, is located in the Texas Medical Center in Houston, TX. Treats patients from all over the world, "Making Cancer History".

Neupogen - medication used to decrease the chance of infection in people who have certain types of cancer and are receiving chemotherapy medications that may decrease the number of neutrophils (a type of blood cell needed to fight infection), in people who are undergoing bone marrow transplants, and in people who have severe chronic neutropenia (condition in which there are a low number of neutrophils in the blood).

Neutropenia - A low number of a specific type of white blood cells called neutrophils. Neutropenia can put some patients at risk for infections and may interrupt chemo treatment. Complications associated with a low white blood cell count are the most common causes of dose reductions or delays in chemotherapy. When a patient is neutropenic, they are typically placed on neutropenic precautions. They must practice good hygiene and avoid contact with people who are sick or have a cold. They must stay away from pets or other animals. They must avoid potted plants or fresh flowers that may carry bacteria in their soil. They must avoid germs through food, by avoiding all fruits and vegetables that cannot be peeled and washed thoroughly. They must wear a mask if they are going to be around others or have others wear a mask around them and they must avoid crowds.

PET Scan - Positron emission tomography (PET) - A nuclear medicine imaging technique that produces a three-dimensional image or picture of processes in the body. It is used to explore the possibility of cancer metastasis (i.e., spreading to other sites).

Platelets - A blood component that aids in clotting. With low numbers of circulating platelets, excessive bleeding can occur.

Red Blood Cells - most common type of blood cell. Functions to deliver oxygen to body tissues. Low levels of circulating red blood cells is called anemia. Anemia can cause fatigue, shortness of breath, weakness, and loss of energy.

Relay for Life - Relay For Life is a life-changing event sponsored by the American Cancer Society that helps communities across the globe celebrate the lives of people who have battled cancer, remember loved ones lost, and fight back against the disease. It is a fundraising event.

TAMU-CC - Texas A&M University Corpus Christi, TX (Lauren's college).

White Blood Cells - blood cells that are involved in the immune system that function to fight infection. If the white blood cells counts are low, you are at increased risk of infection and interruptions in your chemotherapy.

Epilogue

May 28, 2007, will forever be a day I remember. I have almost reached the five-year mark that every cancer patient always wants to reach. In the past five years, I have learned more than I ever expected to know. I have learned that you will find out who your true friends are in a crisis. I have learned that no matter what, you can always count on your family. I have learned that in life's biggest struggles, the best thing you can do is turn to God instead of question Him. I have learned that no one will ever understand what I went through. Everyone's cancer journey is different, regardless of if you are the patient, the caregiver, the family, or the friend. My cancer journey taught me that I have the ability to do anything. I'm not afraid of life like I was before. I no longer worry about where tomorrow will lead me; instead, I live for today. I have learned that even though your world completely stops sometimes, the rest of the world will continue on, with or without you. You have to make that decision if you want to be a part of it.

Cancer is not a death sentence. I became a cancer survivor the day the doctor told me about this disease. Even if cancer takes the life of someone you love, they are a survivor. They survive on through their family and friends, and hopefully those who lose their battle can change the lives of people they knew. People always ask me how I did it, how I got through all the endless cycles of chemotherapy and constant pain and sickness. I didn't do any of it. I trusted that God would get me through it, and He did. Even if my outcome had been different, I would have never stopped trusting Him.

Six years later, I am a happy twenty-six year old! When I was first diagnosed with cancer, I was still trying to decide what to do with my life. Because I didn't want to stop going to school, I tried to find classes that would come easier to me than what I was taking at the time. I graduated from Texas A&M University-Corpus Christi in May 2011 with my Bachelor's degree in Liberal Arts and Communication. Both of my parents work at a local hospital in town, and I have always been led to nursing. I was always fascinated by the stories that my mom would tell me growing up about how the body worked, and I was always amazed by how incredibly smart she was. So I have decided to follow in my mother's footsteps! I recently was accepted into nursing school! I feel that with my experience in hospitals and as a patient can somehow help someone else.

I still have some random side effects from all my cancer treatments, but over the years I've learned to just deal with them. I can't concentrate like I used to. I still don't know if I will ever be able to physically have children. The biggest problem that I have from the cancer is the constant pain. It isn't near what it was before, but the body aches and muscle pains that I have are a constant reminder of what I went through. I have osteopenia, which is the onset of osteoporosis, and parts of my bone in my knees and hips no longer receive blood flow due to all the chemo. I would take these side effects any day, though, because that means that I'm still alive and breathing!

Like I said, I have learned to not take things for granted. I value my family and friends more than I ever have. Although I don't do it enough, I don't feel ashamed or embarrassed to tell them how much I love them or how much they mean to me, because I never know what will happen in my future. There is always a small fear in the back of my mind of the cancer coming back. However, if cancer even knocks on my door again, I'll be ready.

Made in the USA
Columbia, SC
15 September 2020